THE NEW MASS:
A PASTORAL GUIDE

By the same author :

The New Eucharistic Prayers: Text with Commentary (1967)
The New Changes in the Mass (1967)

Contents

Preface

The changes in the Order of Mass over recent years may well be the most important and hazardous enterprise undertaken by the Church in the wake of the Vatican Council.

It is important—because the reshaping of the liturgy is designed to form the Catholic people in the spirituality of Vatican II. All present now take an active part in the liturgy so that all will learn to take an active part in the work of the Church. The new style inculcates the spirit of community, fosters the sense of responsibility to the Church, the Mystical Body of Christ, and so to one another, and to the world which Our Lord came to save.

It is hazardous—because all our religion comes to a focus in the Mass. The liturgy as it was, long standing, familiar, greatly loved, had gathered round it profound and sensitive associations, memories of childhood, first communion, of marriage, of the funerals of parents and friends. To touch this was to risk causing a considerable psychological shock. Would it be stimulating or upsetting? The Church has decided the risk must be taken for the good to be achieved.

The reception of the new style has been, in fact, overwhelmingly favourable. Evidently there have been not a few who have found it hard to change, but even among these there are very many who would greatly miss some of the new features if the clock were turned back to pre-Council days.

The fact is that the new style comes to us with the authority of a General Council of the Church and the personal warrant of the Pope. The proper attitude is therefore not simply to accept but to embrace the new liturgy. As we grow more and more familiar with it, and as the form becomes settled (which everyone longs for), we shall realize that the Holy Spirit is using it to form us in the Christian mould that the new age needs.

The great merit of this book by Father Coughlan is that in it he shows us the reasons both for the changes and for the manner of their introduction. He has been closely associated with the Consilium for the Reform of the Liturgy since its beginnings. He is an enthusiast for the reform and yet has a sensitive and balanced understanding of the problems it involves. I welcome his book and I hope it will be widely read by clergy and laity.

GEORGE PATRICK DWYER
Archbishop of Birmingham

10 October 1969

Introduction

Tales tend to grow in the telling, and the present work, originally intended as a small booklet, is no exception. It attempts to say something useful about why the reform of the Mass has taken the shape it has, and how the new Order of the Mass is actually to be carried out. Its aim is therefore limited. The reader will not find here a full history or theology of the Mass, nor a complete survey of all the rubrics affecting the Mass. But, appearing at a time when the general reform of the Mass is being put into effect, it will, I hope, be of particular service to those who have to present and explain the general reform to others.

For the sake of easy reference, the rubrics given in the General Instruction where it speaks of Mass celebrated with the people, and Mass celebrated without the people, are printed in an Appendix. Throughout the book the abbreviation GI refers to the General Instruction, and OMP to the Order of Mass with the people. The numbering accompanying both abbreviations is that given in the document of 6 April 1969, by which both the Instruction and the Order of the Mass were published by the Holy See.

I should like to thank Fr Gaston Fontaine for his encouragement in writing this book. His commentary on the new lectionary, sent by the Congregation for Divine Worship to the heads of the National Liturgical Commissions, I have been able to use extensively in the present work. My thanks too to Fr John Rotelle and Fr Cormac Murphy O'Connor for their observations, and to those who have in any way helped me in writing this book.

Peter Coughlan
Rome

October 1969

CHAPTER I

The General Reform of the Mass 1964–1969

By 25 January 1959, when Pope John XXIII announced that an Ecumenical Council was to be held, the liturgy was ready for a profound renewal. Over the preceding fifty years or more the liturgical movement had matured and ripened at many levels in the Church.[1] The years following the Second World War had seen the movement grow in intensity. It had already begun to bear fruit in papal pronouncements (Pius XII's *Mediator Dei* being the most important), in practical legislation such as the reforms of Holy Week in the 1950's, and in the books, articles, congresses and study groups on liturgical themes that were beginning to increase in number, particularly in north-western Europe and the United States.

In the words of Pius XII, 'the liturgical movement has appeared as a sign of the providential dispositions of God in the present time, as a passage of the Holy Spirit in his Church',[2] and in the Council the principles of renewal which had come to the fore in this movement found systematic application. The Mass was naturally at the forefront of the Council Fathers' consideration of the liturgy, and the result of the discussion can be

---

[1] For a fuller exposition, cf Herman Schmidt, *Constitution de la sainte liturgie, Editions Lumen Vitae,* Brussels 1966, pp. 49–59.

[2] Pius XII, Address to the First International Congress of Pastoral Liturgy at Assisi, *A.A.S.* 48 (1956) p. 712.

1

found in articles 47–58 of the *Constitution on the Liturgy*.[3] The most important of these is perhaps article 50 :

> 'The rite of the Mass is to be revised in such a way that the intrinsic nature and purpose of its several parts, as also the connection between them, can be more clearly manifested, and that devout and active participation by the faithful can be more easily accomplished. For this purpose the rites are to be simplified, while due care is taken to preserve their substance. Elements which, with the passage of time, came to be duplicated, or were added with but little advantage, are now to be discarded. Where opportunity allows or necessity demands, other elements which have suffered injury through accidents of history are now to be restored to the earlier norm of the holy Fathers.'

The post-Conciliar Commission for the implementation of the Constitution—the Liturgy Consilium as it was called—began work on the reform of the Mass early in 1964. The first fruit of its work was the Instruction of 26 September that year.[4] This was the first stage of the Mass reform. It was obvious that although the general reform would take time to prepare, there were some changes which could be made immediately, and which would meet the demands of the Council Fathers in a practical way. This method of introducing a part only of the reform had the added advantage that it made the renewal a measured one : an important consideration if continuity with the previous celebration of the Mass was to be evident, and if the nature of the changes themselves was to be gradually assimilated and understood.

From the outset, it was intended that the reform should be gradual and should take place by stages, but there were a number of reasons why it sometimes appeared more piecemeal than gradual. For one thing, the groups working on various parts of the Mass did not get through their work at the same speed.

---

[3] The text of *The Constitution on the Liturgy*, and of the major documents regarding liturgical reform since the Council (up to June 1968) may be found in Austin Flannery (ed.), *Liturgy: Renewal and Adaptation*, Sceptre Press, Dublin 1968.

[4] For detailed commentaries on this document, cf J. D. Crichton, *Changes in the Liturgy*, Geoffrey Chapman, London 1965; Frederick McManus, *Sacramental Liturgy*, Herder and Herder, New York 1967.

The revision of the lectionary, for instance, was an enormous task and could not be rushed. Moreover, while some aspects of the reform encountered misunderstanding or opposition, and were delayed, in other aspects the very momentum engendered by the first reforms brought growing demands for further reform. The outstanding example is the progressive extension of the vernacular throughout the Mass. This impression of 'piecemeal' change was accentuated in many places by the lack of adequate preparation and catechesis, and by a succession of changes in translations of the texts already in use. Nevertheless, if we look for a moment at the major changes between 1963 and 1969, we can see how they steadily led up to the new Ordo Missae.

1. THE FIRST POST-CONCILIAR INSTRUCTION :
Inter Oecumenici, 26 September 1964

The 1964 Instruction, following Pope Paul's motu proprio which established 16 February as the date when the Liturgy Constitution was to become law of the Church, began the implementation of what the Fathers of the Council had decided. Its declared purpose was 'to make the liturgy correspond more perfectly with the mind of the Council—to promote, that is to say, the active participation of the faithful' (art. 4). The Instruction then went on to state principles of major importance for the whole of the liturgical renewal :

> 'First of all, however, it is essential that everybody be persuaded that the scope of the *Constitution on the Sacred Liturgy* is not limited merely to the changing of liturgical rites and texts. Rather is its aim to foster the formation of the faithful and that pastoral activity of which the liturgy is the summit and the source (see *Const.*, art. 10). The changes in the liturgy which have already been introduced, or which will be introduced later, have this same end in view' (art. 5).

It declared that the aim of this liturgy-centred pastoral activity is that the paschal mystery of Christ might be expressed in men's lives.

Intelligibility and participation

Five years after its publication, this Instruction remains a fundamental document for those who wish to understand the present liturgical reform. Its main thrust may be summed up under two heads : *intelligibility and participation.*

Intelligibility: the introduction of the vernacular into many parts of the Mass was the effect most forcibly felt in the parishes. This was linked with ceremonial and ritual simplifications which made it easier to see the nature of the various parts of the Mass. The turning round of altars, in many places, to face the people, and the distinction between altar, chair and lectern, further illustrated the character of the different parts of the Mass. Accompanying this was a distinction and distribution of roles, namely, the parts played by the various members of the assembly in the actual celebration. In this way the *participation* of the whole assembly was both facilitated and encouraged, and this in itself was a reflection and image of that sharing of all in the mission of the Church, according to their various roles, which we find in all the documents of the Council.

Intelligibility and participation—these principles had a dynamism of their own, so that once applied in practice, they set in motion a process which has not yet ceased. Time was to show that the translation of one part of the Mass into the vernacular, and the simplification of some of the rites, were to lead to an extension of the vernacular to all the parts of the Mass, and to demands for deeper changes in the Mass's structure. Translating from Latin to English was not enough, since soon came the question : what sort of English? The principles carry us further : in what sort of language should we speak about God today? Inexorably, the question goes on : what do the words and the symbols of the liturgy mean to man today? In England? In India? In the Congo? In Mexico? To different social groups within those countries? We are striking an aspect of that ever-recurring problem in the Church today—the balance between unity and catholicity.

Internal movement of the Mass

There is another aspect of the celebration of Mass which this

Instruction helped to underline, namely its internal movement or development. This is extremely important, since it brings with it a deeper understanding of the part played by the Mass in the Church's life.

'The theology of the counter-Reform insisted above all on the aspects denied by Protestantism : the renewal of the sacrifice of the cross, the eucharistic sacrament of communion, the real presence. These truths have in no sense diminished today, but this approach led to a reflection on the mysterious significance of each moment of the Mass : offertory, consecration, and communion, rather than to a consideration of the "internal movement of the eucharist".'[5]

The present liturgical reform enables us to see these same aspects, these same truths, in a fuller context. It shows more clearly that there is a natural development or rhythm in the Mass, and that its various elements are not just juxtaposed but link and intertwine like the movements of a symphony. We see how the Christian assembly gathers together for the celebration and how the awareness of Christ's presence among them is expressed in the Mass's introductory rites. Gathered together in Christ's name, they listen to the word of God being proclaimed, a proclamation in which Christ's Spirit is present and active in their hearts. The eucharistic liturgy follows almost as a response, a response of praise and thanksgiving, to the proclamation of salvation, the new life, which God offers to men. As the eucharistic rite then unfolds, the whole assembly is gradually drawn more and more into the mystery of Christ which was announced in the reading of the scriptures. His presence among his people attains a new level and depth so that through communion in his Body and Blood those present are taken more fully into his sacrifice, receiving that gift of his Spirit which is the fruit of his death and resurrection. This participation in its turn demands a sharing in Christ's mission in the world, and a 'living out' of this mystery in our lives. Referring to this internal rhythm of the eucharist, Fr Lochet says :

'It is in this "dynamism" of the celebration that we must participate. It is in this very dynamism that we are able to

[5] Louis Lochet, 'Le renouveau de la liturgie eucharistique depuis le Concile', *Nouvelle Revue Théologique* (1969) p. 244.

recognize in the eucharist the efficacious sign, the sacrament, of the Church's unity. This is not a static unity, something complete and ready-made, it is a dynamic unity which is in the process of being made.'[6]

Undoubtedly this is one of the most important aspects of the liturgical renewal. It gives us a renewed insight into the fact that in the gathering of Christians to celebrate the eucharist, the Church is continually coming into being, and continually renewing her mission in the world. It helps us to see the relationship between liturgy and life, and the demands this relationship must inevitably make upon the liturgy itself.

2. CONCELEBRATION AND COMMUNION UNDER BOTH KINDS

The various documents which appeared as the reform progressed gradually underlined further aspects of the part played by the Mass in Christian life. This was certainly true of the document of March 1965, which introduced concelebration. It outlined three qualities very clearly :

'In the first place, the unity of the sacrifice of the cross, for many Masses represent but the one sacrifice of Christ. If they realize the notion of sacrifice, it is because they are the memorial of the bloody immolation accomplished on the cross, whose fruits are received by means of this unbloody immolation.

'Secondly, the unity of the priesthood : since, though many priests celebrate the Mass, all are ministers of Christ who exercises through them his priesthood and, for this end, makes each one of them, by the sacrament of orders, participant in his priesthood in a very special manner. It follows therefore that when each one of them offers the sacrifice, all nevertheless do it in virtue of the same priesthood and act in taking the place of the high priest, to whom it belongs either through one or through many to consecrate the sacrament of his body and his blood.

'Finally, the action of all the people of God is very clearly shown : in fact every Mass, being the celebration of this

[6] *Ibid.*, p. 247.

sacrament by which the Church lives and grows continually and in which the authentic nature of the Church is manifested principally, is more than all the other liturgical actions, the act of all the holy people of God, hierarchically structured and acting.

'Yet, this threefold aspect which belongs to every Mass, is rendered visible in an incomparable fashion in the rite where several priests concelebrate the same Mass.'[7]

The last of these characteristics illustrates yet again the relationship between Church and eucharist, and reminds one of *The Constitution on the Church* when it says

'Incorporated into the Church through baptism, the faithful are consecrated by the baptismal character to the exercise of the cult of the Christian religion. . . . Taking part in the eucharistic sacrifice, which is the fount and apex of the whole Christian life, they offer the divine victim to God, and offer themselves along with it' (art. 11).

Since this is so, every care must be taken when preparing concelebration to ensure the full participation of all present. Thus it will not appear as something peculiarly clerical.

At the same time, communion under both kinds emphasized *B .* another important aspect of the eucharist, namely the aspect of sacred meal or banquet. It is surprising how even today to speak of the Mass as a meal can provoke violent reactions. The reasons for this reaction are perhaps twofold.

The first seems to be the feeling that to speak of the Mass *1)* as a meal would automatically entail a denial of the Mass as a sacrifice. This feeling runs deep. It has its origin in the antagonism between the Protestant Reformation and the Catholic counter-Reform, and history shows that emotional involvement in disputes over religious principles and truth is not something which changes overnight. The fact is of course that the Church has always acknowledged the meal-aspect of the eucharist—it is after all an ineradicable element of the eucharist as instituted by Christ—but historical circumstances have at times caused one aspect to

---

[7] Cf *Liturgy: Renewal and Adaptation*, pp. 60–61.

be stressed more than another. Curiously enough, at a time when Catholics have been giving fuller consideration to the understanding of the Mass as a meal of sacred food and drink, there has been 'a recovery of the sacrificial emphasis in many Protestant theological circles, a witness to which is the statement of the July 1963 meeting of the Faith and Order Conference of the World Council of Churches in Montreal'.[8]

The second reason would seem to be the fear that to speak of the eucharist in this way is automatically to reduce it to a sort of friendship meal without any specifically sacramental significance. But this does not necessarily follow, and to react against real or possible abuses by overstressing one aspect of the truth is to invite equally strong reactions in the other direction. The result is that polarization of opinion and hardening of attitudes to 'left' and 'right' which is a feature of Catholic life at the present time. A contrast of backgrounds, disciplines and attitudes, and a certain tension between them, is often a prerequisite for fruitful development. But when this contrasting of viewpoints hardens into the exclusion of one or the other, growth is stunted. As Fr John Dalrymple has pointed out, we are in danger of 'the all too common Christian phenomenon of two warring points of view within Christianity expending all their energies in debate with each other, while the rest of the world passes by and leaves them to it'.[9]

Our Lord said 'Take this and eat', 'Take this and drink', and for the first twelve centuries the communion of all under both kinds was general practice for those who communicated at Mass. It is still general practice in the Oriental Churches. The reasons for the gradual movement towards reception under one kind in the West are many and complex,[10] but in recent years there has been a growing desire in many countries to return to communion under both kinds when this is a practical possibility. This last point is obviously important—theological principles must always be applied in the light of the practical realities of parish life. The

[8] Frederick McManus, *op. cit.*, p. 95.
[9] John Dalrymple, 'Structures, Persons and Prayer', *Clergy Review,* June 1969, p. 427.
[10] Cf August Franzen, 'Communion under both kinds', *Sacramentum Mundi,,* vol. 1, Burns & Oates, London 1968, pp. 394–6. Clifford Howell, 'Reforming the Liturgy: the Communion Rite, III', *Clergy Review* (August 1968) pp. 626–31.

Council of Trent made three points very clear regarding the reception of communion, namely

a) that the laity and those of the clergy who do not consecrate are not held by reason of divine law to communicate under both species; communion under both species is not necessary for salvation;

b) that the Church has the power to decide whether communion is to be received under one or both species;

c) that Christ whole and entire and the true sacrament are received under each species separately.

Vatican II fully accepted these principles of Trent, but judged that given today's different relationship with the other Christian Churches, and given the development of biblical studies and sacramental theology which illustrated the values of communion under both kinds, it would be good to permit communion under both kinds in certain circumstances. The clearest statement in an official document of the theological reasons for this is the following :

'Holy communion, considered as a sign, has a fuller form when it is received under both kinds. For under this form the sign of the eucharistic banquet appears more perfectly. Moreover, it is more clearly shown how the new and eternal covenant is ratified in the blood of the Lord, as it also expresses the relation of the eucharistic banquet to the eschatological banquet in the kingdom of the Father (cf Mt 26 : 27–29).'[11]

3. MYSTERIUM FIDEI

In September of the same year, 1965, Pope Paul published an encyclical on certain aspects of eucharistic doctrine. This document, *Mysterium fidei,* is a good example of the way Pope Paul has exercised his pastoral office. It is his continual concern that, while encouraging doctrinal development and stimulating pastoral renewal at all levels, he seeks to keep before the minds of the Christian people those aspects of truth and those values of Christian tradition which are in danger of being obscured or neglected. We can see here how the magisterium in the last

[11] Instruction on the Eucharist, 25 May 1967, n. 32.

analysis gives the guarantee of genuine development, since it delineates at least some of those elements which must be taken into account if further insights are to take us to a new level of understanding. The difficulty often lies, however, in determining *how* these same elements are recognizable at this new level of understanding. It is a process which takes time.

In this particular encyclical Pope Paul was concerned with emphasizing the truth of Christ's real presence in the eucharist and the value of former dogmatic formulations with regard to it. He sought also to draw attention to the esteem we should have for the cult of the Blessed Sacrament even outside the celebration of Mass, and to ensure that the highlighting of active participation of all in the Mass did not bring 'private Masses' into disesteem as a result. As is evident from the subsequent documents which he has published on the reform, it was not the Pope's intention to put the brakes on liturgical renewal but rather to keep all those elements in view which go to make up the fullness of Christian faith and worship.

4.   PROGRESS OF THE REFORM

Work had meanwhile continued on the general reform of the Mass, and by October 1965 the first drafts of the new Order of the Mass were ready for the consideration of the bishops of the Consilium.

Perhaps a word about the way the Liturgy Consilium worked would be useful here. The members of this post-Conciliar Commission, set up to implement *The Constitution on the Liturgy,* were appointed directly by the Pope. They were cardinals, archbishops and bishops drawn from all parts of the world, just under fifty in number, chosen either because they were felt to be particularly competent in this field, or because they were heads of the liturgical commissions in their own countries. Many of these bishops had been on the Conciliar Commission for the Liturgy and their inclusion ensured direct continuity with the principles approved by the Council. In addition, there were over two hundred consultors or advisers—the successors to the Council *periti*—and these were divided into study groups treating of the various aspects of the reform. There was also a permanent Secretariat which provided necessary co-ordination of effort, and the head of this was Father Annibale Bugnini, the competent and indefatigable Secretary both of the pre-Conciliar Commission and of the post-Conciliar Commission. The continuity between the Liturgy Consilium's work and the new Congregation for Divine Worship, announced by the Holy Father on 28 April 1969, is underlined by the appointment as its Prefect and Secretary respectively of the former President of the Consilium, Cardinal Benno Gut, and the Secretary, Fr Bugnini. The Consilium continues as a special commission within this Congregation, and will go on until its work of revising the liturgical books, in accordance with the requisites of the Council documents, is complete.

The Consilium normally held plenary sessions twice a year, and it was at the second meeting of the year 1965 that the Mass was submitted to the judgment of the Consilium members. There were practical demonstrations of the Mass as well as discussion on the text, and in general the new form of the Mass met with approval. There were a number of things that were far from complete—the lectionary and the text of the prayers, for example, but the outlines of the new Mass were clear enough. From later discussions it became evident that some bishops wanted the beginning of the Mass to be more carefully considered and that some felt the offertory rite had been simplified too drastically. The question of the canon was particularly difficult. The merits and defects of the Roman Canon have been widely discussed over the last four years and at that time there was discussion as to whether this canon should be simplified and the prayers within it rearranged, or whether it would be better to leave it as it was and compose new canons or eucharistic prayers as alternatives.[12] The question was finally put before the Pope and in 1966 it was decided to adopt the second alternative, namely to draw up new eucharistic prayers to be used in conjunction with the Roman Canon.

While work continued on the Mass reform, its progress was not entirely undisturbed. Often, those who heard of the suggested reforms at fourth or fifth hand received an exaggerated report of what was put forward and seemed to think that this was an

---

[12] For a full discussion of this point and of the reason for adopting the second view, see Cipriano Vagaggini, *The Canon of the Mass and Liturgical Reform*, Geoffrey Chapman, London 1967.

attempt to dismantle the Church's entire liturgy. Naturally, if people thought this was the case, they tended to react violently. It sometimes took time to show that such was not in fact the Consilium's intention, and that there was a direct relationship between what the Council had asked for and what was now being done. These reactions were a useful reminder, if such reminders were needed by those engaged in the reform, that acceptance in theory is one thing but acceptance in practical application is another.

5. THE INSTRUCTION ON MUSIC IN THE LITURGY, 5 March 1967

For some time there had been in preparation two Instructions which were intimately connected with the celebration of Mass, an Instruction on Music in the Liturgy and an Instruction on the Eucharist. The first of these appeared in March 1967, after months of revisions and changes to the original draft. There were considerable differences of opinion among musicians regarding the place of music in the liturgy, and the respective function of choir and congregation. One group pointed to the Church's patrimony of sacred music and the fact that much of it was written for Latin texts. They emphasized the need for it to be sung by adequately prepared people, and fought to resist tendencies which they felt would lead to the abandonment of the riches of the Church's tradition. The other group pointed to the fact that the vernacular would demand a new era of creativity in Church music. They emphasized the need for more active participation by the whole assembly in the singing, and sought to open the door to various types of music. Underlying the differences, perhaps, was a different understanding of the liturgy, and therefore of the function of music in the liturgy.

Happily the Instruction includes positive elements from both points of view, but unhappily the former tensions left their mark on the text itself. As one competent commentator said :

'It exhibits differences of opinion among its compilers which may account for the delay of two and a half years in its publication. The main emphasis is placed squarely on expounding the pastoral implications for music of the Liturgy Constitution, but several paragraphs (seemingly inserted at a very late stage of drafting) modify and at times contradict the main part of the text with the apparent purpose of maintaining the musical *status quo ante*.[13]

One of the most evident examples of the differences within the document may be seen by comparing articles 28–31 (where careful distinctions between different types of sung Mass are laid down and in which it is said that in all types of sung Mass certain parts are always to be sung) with article 36 which says :

'There is no reason why some of the Proper or Ordinary should not be sung in "said" Masses. Moreover, some other song can also on occasion be sung at the beginning, at the offertory, at the communion and at the end of Mass. It is not sufficient, however, that these songs be merely "eucharistic" —they must be in keeping with the parts of the Mass, with the feast, or with the liturgical season.'

The last sentence brings out clearly a fundamental theme of the Instruction. It very strongly encourages greater use of music in the liturgy, urges variety and imagination in choosing and executing it, but stresses always that music must be at the service of the liturgy and not its master. It is perhaps here that we touch the principle bone of contention. As the Abbot Primate of the Benedictines—himself an accomplished musician—has pointed out with regard to some of the Church's musical heritage, 'the compositions we are asked to preserve . . . were the products of a relationship between liturgy and music that is hard to reconcile with the basic premises of the Constitution itself'.[14] And Anthony Milner makes the observation that

'today this "treasury", individual pieces of which seldom secured wide use in their time, is effectively preserved and presented to far larger audiences by radio, records, and concerts, far more effectively than it can be by modern church choirs who use barely one-thousandth part of it'.[15]

[13] Anthony Milner, 'The Instruction on Sacred Music', *Worship* 41 (June–July 1967) p. 322.
[14] Rembert Weakland, 'Music as Art in Liturgy', *Worship* 41 (January 1967) p. 5.
[15] Anthony Milner, *art. cit.*, p. 331.

Main themes of the Instruction

The document has defects, but it has also many positive qualities and merits careful study. It makes quite clear that music is by no means an optional extra in the liturgy. The principle that sung celebrations are the ideal to be striven for underlies the whole document, and is perhaps most clearly expressed in article 27, where it is stated that as far as possible sung celebrations of the Mass are to be preferred. These sung celebrations however are not just left as an ideal to be achieved only by those who have the maximum resources. The Instruction is at pains to stress that many degrees of participation mean that singing is possible even to small groups, and that the music chosen should be suitable to the particular group or assembly. One of the principal reasons for this emphasis on the value of music in the liturgy is well illustrated in the statement of the Music Advisory Board in the United States on 'The Place of Music in Eucharistic Celebrations'.[16] This points out that music, more than any other resource, makes a celebration of the liturgy an attractive human experience. It indicates that the celebration of any liturgical action should be governed by the need for the action to be clear, convincing, and humanly attractive. Succinctly, it declares that

'music must always serve the expression of faith. It affords a quality of joy and enthusiasm to the community's statement of faith that cannot be gained in any other way. In so doing it imparts a sense of unity to the congregation'.

The Music Instruction also develops that differentiation of roles which was a mark of the 1964 Instruction. It delineates the celebrant's role more clearly and illustrates the value of individual cantors or singers who can effectively lead the congregation and proclaim the word of God in song, especially in the psalms sung between the readings. While heavily underlining the people's participation in the singing, it also highlights the role of the choir, which is now more necessary than ever. It describes the choir's dual role : firstly, when it sings alone, and secondly when it fosters, supports and leads the congregation's participation.

The ideal is obviously not that the congregation should sing all the time, nor that the choir should monopolize the singing. On

---

[16] Cf *Crux* Special, 16 February 1968.

this last point the Instruction is explicit. But it is the mind of
the document that *listening, speaking, singing* and *silence* must
all find their place in a well-ordered celebration. Having greatly
stressed the value and necessity of singing by all members of the
assembly, it is interesting to note the importance it gives to
silence :

N.B.

'At the proper times, all should observe a reverent silence.
Through it the faithful are not only not considered as extraneous
or dumb spectators at the liturgical service, but are associated
more intimately in the mystery that is being celebrated, thanks
to that interior disposition which derives from the word of
God that they have heard, from the songs and prayers that
have been uttered, and from spiritual union with the priest in
the parts that he sings or says himself' (art. 17).

Which parts of the Mass should be sung?

With regard to music in the Mass, there remains the practical
point in most parishes and groups : which parts are best sung?
As pointed out above, there is ambiguity in the Instruction on
this point, and a categorical reply is not possible. For the English-
speaking world, we could well turn to the statement approved
by the United States Bishops' Committee for the Liturgy which
was quoted above. As a general principle it states that the best
places to sing are :

A

i)

at the 'Holy, holy, holy'
the acclamations in the middle of the eucharistic prayer
the Amen at its conclusion
the communion song
the responsorial psalm after the first reading and the Alleluia
before the Gospel.
Other places to sing, it says, are :

2)

entrance and dismissal
'Lord, have mercy'
'Glory be to God'
the Lord's Prayer
offertory song.
Many would add the 'Lamb of God' to this list. Its purpose is
to accompany the breaking of bread, and therefore whether it is
said or sung will depend on circumstances.

5)

B.   In choosing the music, apart from the principles outlined above regarding music's relationship to the liturgy, it asks

1)   'Is the music technically and aesthetically good? This question should be answered by competent musicians. This judgment is basic and primary. The musician has every right to insist that the music used be good music; but when this has been determined, there are still further judgments to be made.'

Among other criteria, it gives emphasis to pastoral judgment:

'The pastoral judgment must always be present. It is the judgment that must be made in this particular situation, in these concrete circumstances. Does music in the celebration enable these people to express their faith in this place, in this age, in this culture? A musician may say, for instance, that Gregorian chant is good music. His musical judgment really says nothing about whether and how it is to be used in this celebration. The signs of the celebration must be accepted and received as meaningful. They must, by reason of the materials used, open up to a genuinely human faith experience. This pastoral judgment can be aided by sociological studies of the people who make up the congregation, studies which determine differences in age, culture, and education, as they influence the way in which faith is meaningfully expressed. No set of rubrics or regulations of itself will ever achieve a truly pastoral celebration of the sacramental rites. Such regulations must always be applied with a pastoral concern for the given worshipping community.'

Finally, on this question of pastoral judgment, we might well recall the practical observations of the Commission for Catholic Church Music in England and Wales where it says:

'Varying degrees of solemnity are clearly necessary, and variety of practice can itself be of great pastoral value. In deciding what is to be sung, it may not be out of place to recall that singing is intended to help people, and should therefore not be allowed to become burdensome to them, either through the difficulty of the music chosen, or because of the amount which they are asked to sing. The freedom implicit in the Instruction, however, allows clergy and choirmasters to tackle the problems from a completely practical angle' (No. 4).

6. THE EUCHARISTIC INSTRUCTION, 25 May 1967

The Instruction on the Eucharist was published on 25 May 1967 (two months after the Music Instruction) after a long period of preparation. It remains one of the most important documents published by the Liturgy Consilium. It was intended neither as a compendium of eucharistic theology, nor as a guide to catechetical method. Its aim was primarily practical : to set out major doctrinal principles regarding the eucharistic mystery which should be considered in all instruction upon it, and to state how, in practice, the hierarchy and equilibrium among the various aspects of the eucharist were to be maintained. Since this Instruction could be of great assistance to pastoral priests and teachers in presenting the new Order of the Mass, we shall dwell on it for a moment here.

Doctrinal synthesis

In art. 3 of the Instruction, there is a brief doctrinal synthesis which many readers may find useful. Its content is well illustrated by Fr Tillard, O.P., one of those most closely involved in the document's preparation.[17] He points out that the text begins by emphasizing that the whole sacramental 'organism' has its origin in the Paschal act of the death-resurrection of our Lord, and is prolonged through the Pentecostal gift of his Spirit. Its origin is therefore at one with that of the Church, the body of Christ. But at the heart of this whole 'organism', the eucharist has the privilege of being the memorial of the Paschal event itself, taken up into the dynamic movement of divine love which is its animating force. It is therefore—and this is its essential charac-

[17] J. M. R. Tillard, 'Commentarium', *Notitiae* 31–33 (July–September 1967) p. 263. In the exposition of this article, our text is directly dependent upon this commentary. For further reading on this point cf J. M. R. Tillard, 'Eucharistie et Eglise selon Vatican II', *Parole et Pain* 21 (July–August 1967) pp. 285–309; id., *The Eucharist: Pasch of God's People,* Alba House, New York 1966.

teristic—the memorial of the sacrificial act, accomplished 'once and for all', by which God gives salvation to the world in the death and resurrection of Jesus.

In full fidelity to the desire of Christ, this is achieved in and through the celebration of the supper of the new Passover, the sacramental memorial, which brings the ancient supper of the Jewish Passover to a new level of fulfilment. So it can be stated that the Mass is at one and the same time, and indivisibly, the memorial of the death-resurrection of Christ and the paschal banquet of the new covenant. Receiving the fruits of this sacrifice-banquet in sacramental participation, we partially anticipate, and express our hope in, the eschatological banquet. Since moreover the memorial which is being accomplished is in fact Christ's own sacrifice, sacramentally re-presented without its value of 'once and for all' being in any way compromised, we must conclude that in the Mass the sacrificial aspect and the meal aspect interpenetrate and complement each other in such a way that they are inseparable. On the one hand, the Instruction points out, the sacrifice is only present thanks to the mysterious transformation of the bread and wine over which the eucharist has been pronounced, and on the other hand Christ only makes his own paschal sacrifice present in order to permit the faithful to communicate and share, through sacramental communion in his Body and Blood, in a spirit of faith and love, in the offering of his entire self to the Father.

Three important points should be noted here. Firstly, the rich notion of memorial is put forward for our attention. Properly understood and seen in its biblical context, this notion has the advantage of not isolating the sacrificial aspect from the absolute uniqueness of the historical event to which it refers, a fact which in no way detracts from the truth of the presence of this event in the sacramental act. It therefore implies at one and the same time, and indivisibly, a return in faith to the past event and, by the power of God, the mysterious presence of this event here and now. This all takes places in a context of thanksgiving, praise and intercession without which the memorial does not have its fullness. Another aspect which follows from the first is the emphasis on the profound and structural unity between the sacrificial dimension of the Mass and the eucharistic meal. This counters any tendency to separate them or to give emphasis to

only one of these two elements. A third aspect is the interplay
between Church and Eucharist which is put into clear relief. The
Mass in fact is that act by which the Church relives the mystery
of the Last Supper where Christ himself gave to his own in
sacramental form the Body which was given up for them and
the Blood which was poured out for them. The Mass is thus
revealed as the action of Christ, in his action as our high priest,
and of the Church which, through praise, thanksgiving and intercession, offers herself to the Father in the very act by which she
is taken into the self-offering of her head. That is why every
Mass is a celebration of the Church, head and members. But it
is also the reason why the celebration of Mass is the 'source and
fulfilment' of all eucharistic worship, of all the Church's worship,
of that priestly self-offering which is the faith-life of all the
baptized.

Unity and plurality

From what has been said, it is obvious that the liturgy is very
much bound up with the Church's expression of her own identity.
The liturgy therefore has an intimate role in the individual's
awareness of himself as a Christian, and in his sense of belonging
to the Church.

Given this connection of liturgy with the individual's sense of
belonging to the Church, his sense of security in his faith, it is
not surprising if the advent of more radical change in the liturgy
has been felt by some as a menace to that security and even as a
threat to faith itself. It becomes of maximum importance then
to show the continuity of the new with the old, and to illustrate
the truth that liturgical reform, far from being inimical to a living
faith, is one of its greatest guarantees. As one leading Catholic
sociologist sees it :

'It is probable that the role of the liturgy in the Church
as a social body will continue to increase at the very moment
when a secular, pluralistic and mobile society is offering fewer
opportunities for the automatic transmission of religious values
and norms, and fewer stable forms of belonging that assure
cohesion to the religious group. Ecclesial society must therefore increase its role in these areas through specific action. The
liturgy can play a major part in this evolution if it becomes

more accessible (a channel of communication), more closely linked with the happenings of life (a transmission of values and norms of Christian behaviour), and more diversified (offering multiple forms to manifest the fact of belonging to the Church of Jesus Christ).'[18]

This statement, once accepted, has far-reaching consequences, but here we shall concentrate for a moment on the last point it raises, namely the complex question of the eucharist and *unity*. The eucharist is after all the sacrament of unity, and the Eucharistic Instruction is unequivocal in stating the practical consequences of this:

'Since through baptism "there is neither Jew nor Greek, slave nor freeman, male nor female", but all are one in Christ Jesus (cf Gal 3 :28), the assembly which most fully portrays the nature of the Church and its role in the eucharist is that which gathers together the faithful, men and women, of every age and walk of life' (art. 16).

One of the problems most closely connected with the question of unity is language. The Instruction says:

'Pastors should do what they can to help faithful from other areas join in with the local community. This is above all necessary in city churches and places where many of the faithful come on holiday. Where there are large numbers of emigrants or people of another language, pastors should provide them at least from time to time with the opportunity of participating in the Mass in the way to which they are accustomed. Provision should be made, however, to see that the faithful can say or sing together in Latin those parts of the Ordinary of the Mass that concern them' (art. 19).

In practice, the last point is difficult. On the one hand, there are people who have a marked preference for the Latin Mass as they have known and cherished it over the years. As far as manpower, resources, and conflicting pastoral needs allow, provision must be made for these people, particularly in large city churches which are easily accessible by public transport. Likewise,

[18] François Houtart, 'Sociological Aspects of the Liturgy', *Worship* 42 (June–July 1968) p. 347.

the value of everyone being able to sing at least the Ordinary of the Mass in Latin is evident at international gatherings and places of pilgrimage. While this is desirable in theory, the speed with which Latin has dropped out over the last few years makes one wonder to what extent it will remain in the realm of theory. This is particularly the case with the countries outside Europe and North America. Canon Houtart expresses the viewpoint of the great majority of young intellectual Christians of the ex-colonial countries when he says:

'Undoubtedly, the primary concern that governed the preservation of Latin in the liturgy was the desire to manifest the unity of the rite throughout the Church (at least the Latin Church). This is certainly a value to safeguard, but by more appropriate means. Unity of language amounted to the imposition of a unity of culture and hence in the end contradicted universality. . . . The accent must be placed on the one Lord that all peoples revere in their own tongue and in accordance with their own culture. This is a much more fundamental value.'[19]

In harmony with this viewpoint, there is the growing desire in some areas for liturgical forms which are more closely related to local culture. Examples of this were seen at the East Asian Conference on Catechetics and Liturgy held in Manila, Philippines, 1967, and at the National Catholic Seminar in Bangalore, India, 1969. These aspirations would certainly seem valid if Christianity is to become truly 'incarnate' in these countries. On the other hand, unity is a value to safeguard, and this even more so in a world where communications and mobility are making the globe smaller and making men more immediately present to one another. All around the world, men watched man's effort to reach the moon, and Colonel McDivitt, astronaut of Apollo IX, once remarked that, looking back towards earth on the way to the moon, 'it is the unity of the earth which strikes you from up there; divisions and frontiers disappear'. At such a time, when the need for international organization and co-operation is becoming each day more evident, every care must be taken to ensure that the celebration of the eucharist does not become a sign of disunity. Perhaps a multiplicity and flexibility of forms of

[19] François Houtart, *art. cit.*, p. 363.

celebration is the only way of meeting these different needs, but this 'unity in diversity' must always be open to, leading towards, the celebration of the eucharist by all members of the Church, irrespective of nationality, rite, etc. An example of this was the same Indian Seminar mentioned above when on the closing day bishops and priests of different rites and regions concelebrated Mass together with all the participants gathered around the altar —a witness, said Archbishop Mar Gregorios of the Syro-Malankara rite, that 'the Spirit of love has come down upon us'. The eucharist must always be an effective witness to that fact.

There is another aspect of unity and multiplicity of form in the Mass that is causing widespread discussion at the present time, namely the celebration of the eucharist by different types of groups within the same society. Many feel that the celebration of the liturgy must be more adaptable to specific groups of people. It would seem reasonable, for example, to adapt the Mass in one way for celebration in the living-room of private homes, and in another way for celebration in St Peter's Square. It would seem advisable to adapt the Mass in one way for ten-year-olds, and in another way for university graduates. Just as the ways of belonging to the Church have diversified more in modern society, so too it seems necessary for the liturgy to meet the needs of different groups. Canon Houtart points out that in each case the nature of the social group must be respected. The small group, for example, can be of great importance in helping to create a sense of belonging and can foster a more intimate participation. But this does not mean that the same pattern of direct inter-personal relations proper to the small group can or should be imposed on the normal parish assembly. This larger assembly has a more public quality, and is characterized by a greater formalization of roles (but not *formalism*), and standardization of actions and words to give the celebration a more 'universal' appeal. Moreover,

'the individual who participates in the assembly may not want to be integrated into small-group relationships. There is obviously no objection to the assembly's giving various small groups the opportunity to come together or to form under its aegis. But the two realities must not be confused. There are many ways of giving the assembly a more personal character,

without seeking to transform it into a social reality that is alien
to its nature.'[20]

It is clear also that the participation required at eucharistic congresses where thousands of people are present, or at places of
pilgrimage such as Lourdes, is different again from that of the
parish.

Considering these groups from the point of view of the
eucharist as 'sacrament of unity', there is another observation
which goes to the heart of the matter : the small group must never   N. 13.
be cut off from its reference to the larger community.

> 'To identify the liturgical act with the social dimension of
> the small group would involve the risk of forming closed
> societies which would quickly develop exclusive values and
> become intransigent on the same basis as religious sects.
> Mechanisms must be found to avoid such excecesses—for
> example, careful training and permanent contact with those
> who have the responsibility of presiding over the liturgical
> act, or perhaps orientation towards a larger community that
> clearly manifests the non-exclusive social character of the
> Catholic group. Moreover, the concerns of the group must
> always be orientated toward the universal community.'[21]

It follows, of course, that the parish must also look beyond its
own boundaries, as it will if it is imbued with a Christian sense
of mission.

The eucharist as 'sacrament of unity' is something which comes
up in almost all discussions upon the eucharist, but to date the
sociological dimension of this question has received too little
attention in the liturgical renewal. If we are to see how a true
'unity in catholicity' is to be achieved in the coming years, we
would do well to give it more consideration in the future.

Mass and reservation

The Instruction goes on to give further general norms (e.g.
regarding the celebration of one Mass at a time so as not to
disperse the congregation's attention and participation; the distri-

[20] François Houtart, art. cit., p. 362.
[21] François Houtart, art. cit., p. 361.

bution of communion; the place of the Mass in the life of bishops and priests, etc.) and then treats of the worship due to the Blessed Sacrament reserved. If we are to try to keep all values in balance, we must consider this question for a moment. Devotion to the Blessed Sacrament has been most fruitful in helping many to deepen that personal relationship with Christ and that sharing in his mission which is after all the very goal of liturgical reform. In our own day it continues to be at the heart of the spirituality of many religious congregations and movements—among them the followers of Peter Emyard and the followers of Charles de Foucauld and Père Voillaume. It also touches on the extremely important point of the relationship between the liturgy and personal prayer.

The Instruction outlines the relationship between the celebration of Mass and the reservation of the Blessed Sacrament, and it will help us to see the reservation of the Blessed Sacrament in perspective if we follow through its line of thought.[22]

Pervading the entire Instruction is the principle that all eucharistic worship and devotion is centred on the celebration of the Mass, and should be seen as leading up to or flowing from this celebration. It follows that the lay-out of a church should foster the fullest and deepest participation in the Mass. In particular, this means that the three focal-points of the action of the Mass should be seen as such. These three focal-points are the celebrant's chair, the lectern, and the altar. A word on the placing of these three centres of attention may be useful.

It is often suggested that the celebrant's chair should be at the centre of the rear wall and looking out across the altar towards the congregation. In small churches, or in churches where the people are gathered in a fan-shape around the altar, this can be a good solution. In large churches, however, and especially in churches which are long and narrow, this arrangement makes the priest too distant from the people. The best arrangement will often be to have the *chair* to the side and slightly forward of the altar. The main advantage of this is that it ensures a more immediate contact between the priest and congregation. The best position for the *lectern* is often parallel to the position just mentioned for the chair, but on the other side of the altar; the church's acoustics

---

[22] Cf Peter Coughlan, 'The Celebration of Mass and the Reservation of the Blessed Sacrament', *Adoremus* (July 1968), pp. 89–92.

however may demand a different solution. The *altar* should be ³⁾
seen to be *the* natural focus of attention in the church. But at
the same time it should not be so placed as to appear distant and
unapproachable. It is around the altar that the Christian family
gather to celebrate the memorial of the Lord, offering themselves
together with Christ and coming to his table to receive the bread
of life. From this point of view, the arrangement where the seats
of the congregation are positioned in a fan-shape around the
altar, and in which the rows of seats slope down progressively
towards the altar, is often a good one.

The tabernacle is not a focal point in the action of the Mass
and in fact the reservation of the Blessed Sacrament finds its
principal purpose outside the Mass. Where then should it be
placed?

The Instruction states that when Mass is being celebrated, it is
better that the Blessed Sacrament should not already be present
on the altar :

> 'In the celebration of Mass the principal modes of worship
> by which Christ is present to his Church are gradually re-
> vealed. First of all, Christ is seen to be present among the
> faithful gathered in his name; then in his word, as the scrip-
> tures are read and explained; in the person of the minister;
> finally, and in a unique way, under the species of the eucharist.
> Consequently, because of the sign, it is more in keeping with
> the nature of the celebration that the eucharistic presence of
> Christ, which is the fruit of the consecration and should be
> seen as such, should not be on the altar from the very begin-
> ning of Mass through the reservation of the sacred species in
> the tabernacle' (art. 55).

Quite apart from the theological reasons, when Mass is celebrated
on an altar facing the people—and this is increasingly the case—
having a tabernacle on the altar hinders the view of the celebrant's actions. Where then should the tabernacle be placed? The
Instruction's reply to this is not categorical, but it states a
preference :

> 'It is recommended that, as far as possible, the tabernacle
> be placed in a chapel distinct from the middle or central part
> of the church' (art. 53).

It would seem that the following points should be borne in mind :

a) Where possible, there are many practical reasons for wanting to ensure that the tabernacle is easily accessible from the altar. In No. 49 the Instruction also says :

'It would be well to recall that the primary and original purpose of the reserving of the sacred species in church outside Mass is the administration of the Viaticum.'

b) 'The place in a church or oratory where the Blessed Sacrament is reserved in the tabernacle should be truly prominent.'

c) 'It ought to be suitable for private prayer so that the faithful may easily and fruitfully, by private devotion also, continue to honour our Lord in this sacrament' (art. 53).

This last point is important and largely explains the preference expressed in the Instruction for a Blessed Sacrament chapel. The aim is that there should be that intimacy and tranquillity which will encourage personal prayer. In my own opinion it is also desirable that the tabernacle should be so placed that the faithful are easily aware when they enter the church of where the Blessed Sacrament is, and moreover that the place of reservation should be readily accessible.

There are nevertheless many cases when, due to the size or shape of the church, it is neither possible nor desirable to have a Blessed Sacrament chapel. But the principles outlined above still apply when considering where the Blessed Sacrament is to be reserved. One of the solutions often adopted when rearranging the sanctuary so as to have the altar facing the people, is to place the tabernacle against the centre of the rear wall of the sanctuary. According to the words of the Instruction, this is not the ideal solution, but there are a good number of cases where it is the only practical one. This is especially true of small chapels, and of churches which are long and narrow.

In a carefully worded article, the Eucharistic Instruction underlines the nature and value of private devotion to the Blessed Sacrament :

'When the faithful adore Christ present in the sacrament, they should remember that this presence derives from the sacrifice and is directed towards both sacramental and spiritual communion.

'In consequence, the devotion which leads the faithful to visit the Blessed Sacrament draws them into an even deeper participation in the paschal mystery. It leads them to respond gratefully to the gift of him who through his humanity constantly pours divine life into the members of his body. Dwelling with Christ our Lord, they enjoy his intimate friendship and pour out their hearts before him for themselves and their dear ones, and pray for the peace and salvation of the world. They offer their entire lives with Christ to the Father in the Holy Spirit and receive in this wonderful exchange an increase in faith, hope and charity. Thus they nourish those right dispositions which enable them with all due devotion to celebrate the memorial of the Lord and receive frequently the bread given us by the Father.

'The faithful should therefore strive to worship Christ our Lord in the Blessed Sacrament, in harmony with their way of life. Pastors should exhort them to this, and set them a good example' (art. 50).

In the long run the liturgical reform will not achieve the effects it seeks if it is not accompanied in the lives of those taking part by an awareness of God's presence and action, and by a responsiveness to this action, i.e. if there is not a spirit of personal prayer. Just because the Mass is the high-point of the Church's sacramental life, it does not follow that all other forms of prayer and devotion become irrelevant or unnecessary. Both public prayer and personal communion with God are part of a full Christian life. Pope Paul recently remarked that :

'the liturgy, the public and official worship of the Church, is neither a substitute for, nor an impoverishment of, personal religion. On the contrary, personal religion is the indispensable condition of authentic and aware participation in the liturgy. It is indeed the fruit, the consequence of this participation in the liturgy which is intended precisely to sanctify souls and to anchor within them the sense of union with God, with Christ, with the Church and with the brotherhood of men.'[23]

[23] Allocution at the General Audience of 13 August 1969, quoted in *The Tablet*, 23 August 1969, p. 843.

7. THE SECOND INSTRUCTION, *Tres abhinc annos*, 4 May 1967

In 1967 there also appeared what was called the 'Second Instruction' or 'Tres abhinc annos'.[24] It takes us back to the actual reform of the Mass which had been going on in the previous years. We saw earlier that it had been provisionally decided in 1966 to work on the preparation of alternatives to the Roman Canon, and it was again on the canon that the spotlight fell in the latter months of that year and throughout 1967. The immediate cause of this was the American hierarchy's request that the canon of the Mass be allowed to be said out loud and in the vernacular. Other hierarchies were not slow to follow their lead. The reasons presented were straightforward : experience with the vernacular had naturally led to a desire that the canon, the heart of the Mass, should also be intelligible. What is more, had not St Paul said 'Whenever you do this, you proclaim the death of the Lord until he comes?' The canon, or eucharistic prayer, *is* that proclamation ! It is reasonable, they said, that the canon should in fact recover its proclamatory character—in the vernacular and out loud. This was backed up by the facts of liturgical history. In Rome the canon began to be said in Latin instead of Greek about the middle of the third century. Why? Because many of the people could no longer understand Greek—the first vernacular movement ! By the eighth century, most of the people in western Europe no longer understood Latin, and the canon gradually began to be said silently by the priest, who understood the Latin, while the people listened to the singing of the choir. It was inevitable that the renewed understanding of the eucharistic prayer as a proclamation of God's action among his people—past and present—would in time bring a return to the vernacular, and even to new eucharistic prayers which would more fully express our understanding of God's action amongst us today.

The introduction of the vernacular canon largely explains this 'Second Instruction', which brought many simplifications in the rubrics regarding the canon—genuflections, kisses of the altar, signs of the cross, etc. At the same time, however, it also met

---

[24] For a detailed commentary on this Instruction, cf Peter Coughlan, *The New Changes in the Mass*, Geoffrey Chapman, London 1967.

the requests of many bishops regarding the choice of Mass formularies, simplifications in the divine office, the rites for the dead and the use of liturgical vestments. It was called the 'Second' Instruction since it was in direct continuation with that of September 1964. Aware of the difficulties of pastoral clergy amid the seas of change, the text said of the changes 'on the one hand they are judged to be useful in the gradual introduction of liturgical renewal, and on the other they can be applied by rubrics which do not demand changes in the liturgical books at present in use'. The changes which *did* affect the liturgical books were soon to go before the Synod.

8. THE SYNOD OF BISHOPS, *October 1967*

It was Pope Paul's desire that the main points of liturgical reform be submitted to the judgment of the bishops of the world before going into effect. Accordingly, the drafts of the new Order of the Mass were put before the bishops at the Synod of October 1967. Besides an exposition of the contents and guiding principles of the revision, there was also a 'demonstration Mass'.

This Mass was celebrated in the Sistine Chapel on 24 October. It was presented as an example of a normal Sunday Mass in an Italian parish, with the people participating, with a choir, a reader, a cantor and two altar servers. The readings were taken from the new lectionary, and the chants from the Simple Gradual. All present had booklets with the texts and music to help them participate. There were, however, one or two factors which militated against this being accepted as a 'normal parish Mass'.

The setting, with Michelangelo's Christ of the Last Judgment exploding in glory from the far wall, the power and beauty of the creation scene above, the classical harmony and repose of Botticelli and Ghirlandaio frescoes down the walls, coupled with an awareness that it was here the cardinals had so often gathered to elect the successors of St Peter, made for a rather unusual parish church. The congregation—with sixty-three cardinals and over a hundred archbishops and bishops—and Cardinal Ottaviani leading the way in the prayers of the faithful, was not entirely typical of the normal congregation. The choir, by reason of its preparation and competence, was certainly way ahead of most parish choirs. It is understandable, then, that while the general reaction was favourable, there were some—and among them a goodly sample of Anglo-Saxons and Celts—who felt a little uneasy as they set this against the background of early Sunday morning Masses at home, with the fog and drizzle swirling around the church doors and children sneezing and crying in the pews.

The title given to this revision was the 'normative Mass' and this only aggravated their unease. At this Mass all the singable parts had in fact been sung. Was normative meant in the strict sense, that it should be done in all parish Masses on a Sunday? The idea was unthinkable. And they said so! The Consilium spokesman went to great pains in the following days to explain that a good deal of flexibility was intended within the structure of this new Mass, and that there was variety—from the Mass at which nothing or almost nothing was sung, to a Mass in which all the singable parts were sung and with various types of music. It was pointed out that there were varying degrees of solemnity in the new Mass, and that variety was positively encouraged. They had to agree however that the phrase 'normative Mass' was rather a misnomer, and it has nowhere appeared in the 1969 documents.

The overall voting of the bishops was undoubtedly favourable to the new Order of the Mass, but the suggested amendments were many and varied.[25] As the meetings of the Consilium later showed, it was difficult to reconcile the different viewpoints expressed. It was impossible in fact to revise the Mass in such a way as to please everybody; inevitably then there had to be give and take, and an element of compromise.

Some felt that the offertory had been stripped down too far, and accordingly in the revisions following the Synod some texts were re-inserted. Others felt that it would be too much for all three readings at the beginning of Mass to be obligatory, and so while it is still strongly encouraged that the three readings be used, only two are in fact obligatory—unless the local hierarchy decides otherwise. Other changes too were made in the light of the Synod.

One striking aspect of the speeches and suggestions in the Synod was the differing attitudes of bishops from different areas. Some African-born bishops, for example, spoke of the need for

[25] For a detailed account of the voting of the bishops at the Synod, cf *Notitiae* 35 (November 1967) pp. 353–80.

colour, movement and music in their liturgy. Some of the English-speaking bishops underlined the value of silence and recollection, the difficulties of singing and the need for a period of calm in liturgical renewal. Bishops from north-western Europe, where the liturgical renewal had its origins, wanted further simplicity of line and clarity of structure so that the meaning might be evident, flexibility within the rite and the possibility of adaptation to small groups and children. Bishops from South America differed widely in their attitudes, as did the bishops from Asia. Some wanted more experimentation in concrete situations and a greater degree of adaptation, while others shied away from the very idea of experimentation, feeling that it heralded chaos.

Against such a background, the work of the Liturgy Consilium in preparing the final text for publication was not easy, and in fact the final decisions were not those of the Consilium alone. As this work progressed in 1968, it was felt that one extremely important item, which had met the overwhelming support of the bishops at the Synod, could be introduced : the new eucharistic prayers and prefaces.[26] The great advantage of introducing these straightaway was that it provided the opportunity for catechesis to concentrate on this aspect of the Mass and, further, to prepare the way for the new Order of the Mass itself. The introduction of these new eucharistic prayers is one of the most important reforms to date, and we shall return to it when commenting on the new Order of the Mass itself.

9. THE 1969 DOCUMENTS

We come now to the series of documents published in 1969, which effect the general reform of the Mass—the completion of the work which the 1964 Instruction had begun. It will be useful to present the documents briefly.

In an Apostolic Constitution, *Missale Romanum,* dated 3 April 1969, Pope Paul VI approved the new Missal as revised according to the directives of Vatican II, and authorized its publication. Two major documents were then published simultaneously : the

---

[26] Cf Peter Coughlan, *The New Eucharistic Prayers,* Geoffrey Chapman, London 1967; Gerard J. Broccolo, *Let Us Give Thanks,* Chicago Archdiocese Liturgy Commission, 1967.

new Order of the Mass, and the accompanying *Institutio Generalis,* a general instruction with 8 chapters and 341 articles, which replaces the former 'General rubrics', 'Rite to be followed in the celebration of Mass' and 'Defects which can occur in the celebration of Mass'. Bearing the date of 6 April, these documents were to go into effect on the first Sunday of Advent 1969.

Following closely on these two documents came the new lectionary : this contains the readings for Sundays and feasts of the temporal cycle, for weekdays or ferias, for the Proper and Common of the Saints, for Ritual Masses (such as marriages and ordinations), for Votive Masses and for Masses for Various Occasions.

Completing the publication of the new Missal and appearing later in 1969 came the document containing the revision of the prayers (collects, prayer over the gifts, prayer after communion) and antiphons (entrance and communion), together with seventy new prefaces for use in the eucharistic prayer.

Closely connected with the new Order of the Mass, and profoundly modifying the Roman Missal, is the publication of the new calendar of the Church's year, in which both the temporal cycle and the sanctoral cycle have been revised.

The *General Instruction* or *Institutio Generalis* is a considerable improvement on the documents it replaces and is well worth careful attention. In our presentation of the new Mass in the next chapter, we shall be drawing on it frequently, but it may be useful here to indicate its contents.

The document contains eight chapters. The first is an introduction of doctrinal character. The second reviews the various elements of the celebration giving the doctrinal and rubrical presentation of each. The third illustrates the roles of each of those participating in the celebration : priest, people and ministers. The fourth sets out the various forms of celebration : Mass with the people, private Mass, concelebrated Mass; and also contains norms for communion under both species. The fifth offers an ample set of directives on the arrangement of the church as a place of celebration. The sixth reviews what is needed for the celebration : furnishings, instruments, and vestments. The seventh gives guidance in choosing the formulary of the Mass and its various parts : readings, chants, prayers, offering a series of possible adaptations and a number of different forms. The eighth summarizes in two pages the hitherto very wide and extremely complicated legislation on Votive Masses and Masses for the Dead.

As can be seen, this is a document with a clear linear structure, inspired by pastoral principles, and intended as an aid and guide rather than as a series of rules.

CHAPTER II

The New Order of the Mass: Introductory

1. SOME GENERAL POINTS

'The celebration of Mass, as the action of Christ and of the people of God structured hierarchically, is the centre of the entire Christian life both for the Church, local and universal, and for each of the faithful. In the Mass, we have the apex of the action by which God sanctifies the world in Christ, and of the worship which men show to the Father, adoring him through Christ the Son of God. Moreover, in this sacred action the mysteries of redemption are recalled in the gradual unfolding of the year, and in a certain sense are made present. All other sacred actions and all the works of the Christian life are linked with it, flow out from it, and lead back to it' *(Institutio Generalis, 1).*[1]

The whole of this book is a commentary on that statement, but there are a few ideas which we could well look at before studying the Mass itself.

(i) *The action of Christ*

The first is the understanding of the Mass as the action of Christ in our midst. This requires *faith.* An awareness through

[1] Hereafter referred to as GI.

34

faith of Christ's presence is the *sine qua non* of Christian worship. It is the atmosphere without which there is no Christian life—it is like the air without which we cannot breathe. An excellent illustration of the relationship between faith and the celebration of Mass is given in the statement prepared by the Music Advisory Board of the United States, to which we referred earlier. It says :

'We are Christians because through the Christian community we have met Jesus Christ, heard his word of invitation, and responded to him in faith. We assemble together at Mass in order to speak our faith over again in community and, by speaking it, to renew and deepen it. We do not come together to meet Christ as if he were absent from the rest of our lives. We come together to deepen our awareness of, and commitment to, the action of his Spirit in the whole of our lives at every moment. We come together to acknowledge the work of the Spirit in us, to offer thanks, to celebrate.

'People in love make signs of love and celebrate their love for the dual purpose of expressing and deepening that love. We too must express in signs our faith in Christ and each other, our love for Christ and for each other, or they will die. We need to celebrate.

'We may not feel like celebrating on this or that Sunday, even though we are called by the Church's law to do so. Our faith does not always permeate our feelings. But this is the function of signs in the Church : to give bodily expression to faith, to transform our fragile awareness of Christ's presence in the dark of our daily isolation to a joyful, integral experience of his liberating action in the solidarity of the celebrating community.

'From this it is clear that the manner in which the Church celebrates the liturgy has an effect on the faith of men. Good celebrations foster and nourish faith. Poor celebrations weaken and destroy faith.'

(ii) *And of the people of God*

The second point is that this faith—this celebration of the Mass by the local community—does not exist in a vacuum. The Mass is the centre of Christian life—but surely that means that this life is Christian! A remarkable grasp of the obvious? Unless the community worshipping at Mass is conscious, at least to some extent, of a shared purpose in life, a purpose and meaning which actually makes demands upon and transforms that life in a way shared by all those worshipping, then it does not really make much sense to talk about a Christian community at worship. Worship in the Church's liturgy must find its corresponding 'worship' in life or else it is dead.

I once heard the parish described as 'an outward-looking worshipping community with a Christian social purpose', and this description is very much to the point here. 'Social purpose' is a term which extends to all the forms that result from the witness Christians give to Christ's saving presence in the world, and this 'witness' is something which Christians share according to the circumstances of their lives. It is the concrete expression of the worship they offer in the eucharist. Conversely, the eucharist gives significance and meaning to that life and is a source of its strength, for it is in the Church's liturgy that we have direct contact with the life-giving humanity of the Son of God made man. If Christ's incarnation extends through human history in his body, the Church, then this is above all true of the eucharist in which, according to the teaching of the Second Vatican Council, the Church has its principal expression.

This Church is *hierarchically structured*. It is not a question of who has the higher or lower position, it is a question of what function the Spirit has given to each, because 'just as each of our bodies has several parts and each part has a separate function, so all of us, in union with Christ, form one Body, and as parts of it we belong to each other. Our gifts differ according to the grace given us' (Rom 12 :4–5). This will entail that each acts according to the sacramental grace—of baptism, of baptism and order—he has received, and according to the personal gifts and talents he has been given. This is that 'shared responsibility' about which we have heard so much recently, in which the obligations and responsibilities of each one are recognized and accepted, and the exercise of these responsibilities are positively encouraged.

This differentiation of function is reflected in the celebration of the eucharist through the distribution of roles, and the harmonious participation of all in the liturgical action. The role of each person should be carefully worked out in the actual celebration : the role of the celebrant, the deacon, the lector, the psalmist or cantor, the choir, the organist, the altar-servers or ministers, the commentator, the apparators or ushers, and the role of the general congregation of the faithful. All have a specific role in the Mass, and these roles must be ordered and co-ordinated according to the requirements of each particular celebration.

(iii) *The importance of place*

The third point is that the place where the Christian community gathers to celebrate Christ's presence should be adapted to the celebration.

'Just as the language we use conditions us, so the space and light in which we live and move, and the forms and colours that strike our eyes, influence our modes of perception and our receptivity. They therefore also affect our attitudes and modes of behaviour. In preparing for a fruitful celebration of the liturgy we cannot afford to ignore these facts. The building in which the liturgy takes place, the artistic forms used, the variety and quality of the music, the arrangement of the place of worship, all the things which affect our sense faculties must be carefully chosen if they are to express the meaning of the liturgy and lead to an awareness of God's presence among us. Language and symbol are interpenetrated in the liturgy, just as ideas and sentiments are inextricably intertwined in the daily lives and attitudes of the people for whom the liturgy is celebrated. This must be borne in mind, because if the liturgy is to elicit a total response from the people taking part then it must be addressed to the whole person.'[2]

2. THE 'TYPICAL' MASS

The Mass we shall be considering in these pages will be that primarily considered by the General Instruction and the new Order of the Mass—namely, 'Mass celebrated with the people'. Based on article 41 of the *Constitution on the Liturgy,* which stated that the rite of the Mass was to be reformed 'bearing in

[2] Adalberto Mª Franquesa, 'Presentacion de la neuva Ordenacion General del Missal Romano'. *Phase* 51 (1969) p. 224.

mind Masses which are celebrated together with the people', the emphasis in the new Mass is not on the solemnity of form or on what parts are sung, but on the active participation of the assembly. Accordingly the new Order of Mass begins with the mention of the assembled people (GI, 77), and ends with their dismissal. For this reason, the Mass proposed as the model or type is that in which :

the celebration includes song and the people themselves sing;

in which there is a suitable number of 'ministers' or servers, normally including a lector;

there is a choir, or at least a cantor.

Other celebrations of Mass, with or without singing, are to be related to this as to their model, and are either amplifications or restrictions of this basic form.

The Mass reform also sought to make the two principal parts of the Mass, the liturgy of the word and the eucharistic liturgy, stand out as distinct from one another, and yet so closely linked as to form one act of worship. Our consideration of the Mass will thus be primarily concerned with these two principal elements, but we shall also be considering the rites which introduce the Mass and close it.

There are two preliminary points affecting the whole Mass which can be given most conveniently here :

(i)   *Standing, kneeling, sitting*

When the same bodily posture is adopted by all those taking part in the liturgy it is a sign of the cohesion and unity of the assembly (GI, 20). It can help to express and foster their active participation. If the celebration is to be well ordered and co-ordinated, all present should follow the directions regarding standing, sitting and kneeling given by the presiding priest, by the deacon, or by the minister assigned this task (GI, 21). The General Instruction further states that 'it is for the Episcopal Conference to adapt the gestures and bodily positions described in the Order of the Roman Mass to the character and customs of their people'. It adds that care should be taken to ensure that these adaptations are suited to the nature and significance of each part of the celebration (GI, 21). Some writers have sought to give theological reasons for the variety of postures during the Mass, but the value of such 'theology' is limited.

The general pattern in the English-speaking world, adapting present usage to the new Order of the Mass, would probably be as follows :

a) from the entrance hymn to the end of the collect : *standing*
b) from the first reading to the beginning of the Alleluia or Gospel : *sitting*
c) from the Alleluia to the end of the Prayers of the Faithful : *standing*
d) from the presentation of gifts to the Orate fratres : *sitting*
e) from the Orate fratres to the end of the Sanctus : *standing*
f) from the end of the Sanctus to the end of the eucharistic prayer : *kneeling*
g) from the introduction of the Lord's Prayer to the prayer before communion : *standing*
h) at the Ecce Agnus Dei and during communion : *kneeling*
i) at the silent thanksgiving after communion : *sitting*
j) from the Postcommunion to the end of Mass : *standing*.

In some places, of course, there is already a custom of standing both during the eucharistic prayer and at communion—a custom sometimes dictated not merely by general attitudes but by force of circumstance ! The General Instruction suggests standing from the prayer over the gifts until the end of Mass, with the exception of sitting during the silent thanksgiving, and kneeling during the consecration. The idea of standing all the time may be too much for many of the older members of the congregation. Moreover, the suggestion of genuflecting just for the consecration is open to criticism. Surely it would be better to kneel all the way through the eucharistic prayer, or to stand all the way through it? Quite apart from the distraction caused by the clattering of benches, placing of trouser creases and arranging of skirts as people kneel at this point, the action seems to cut across the essential unity of the prayer itself.

With regard to general practice, it is obviously reasonable that the Italians and Dutch should not force their customs in this regard on one another, and eminently reasonable that neither should impose their Western habits on India and Japan. On the other hand, there should be consistency within the same parish as to when people stand, sit and kneel, and there are evident reasons for establishing a consistent pattern throughout a country so that people feel easily 'at home' when they go to Mass in another parish or diocese. Personally I feel that while intelligent adaptation and wholesome variety are to be strongly encouraged, we should try and avoid any pattern of 'high church' and 'low church' emerging from the present liturgical renewal. Greater freedom and adaptability in bodily posture is clearly necessary when Mass is not celebrated in church.

(ii)   *The use of incense*

'Incense may be used in any form of Mass :
a)   during the entrance procession
b)   at the beginning of Mass to incense the altar
c)   at the procession and proclamation of the Gospel
d)   at the offertory, to incense the gifts, altar, priest and people.

The priest puts incense into the thurible, and blesses it with a sign of the cross, saying nothing.

The incensation of the altar is done in this way :

a)   if the altar is separate from the wall, the priest incenses it as he goes round it
b)   if the altar is not separate from the wall, the priest moves in front of it incensing first the right side, and then the left side of the altar. If the cross is on the altar or by the side of it, it is incensed before the altar; if it is behind the altar, the priest incenses it when he crosses in front of it' (GI, 235, 236).

CHAPTER III

The Entrance
and Introductory Rites

'The actions and prayers which precede the liturgy of the word, namely the entrance song, the greeting, the penitential act, the Kyrie, the Gloria, and the prayer (collect), have the character of an opening, introduction and preparation' (GI, 24).

The purpose of these rites is to unite the assembled faithful and to help them to become conscious of themselves as a community. Through these rites the faithful prepare themselves to listen carefully to the word of God and to celebrate the eucharist worthily (GI, 24).

It is evident from this that the entrance rites are secondary to the liturgy of the word, and should be so designed as to lead into it reasonably swiftly. This was the fundamental idea in the minds of those preparing the reform. Any solemn community act will begin with an introduction and greeting, but over the course of time this part of the Mass had become lengthy and complicated, often lasting longer than the liturgy of the word itself. At a sung Mass, for example, the *Asperges* was followed by the singing of the Introit antiphon (by the choir), the prayers at the foot of the altar by the reciting of the Introit antiphon by the celebrant, the Kyrie and the Gloria (often sung to lengthy polyphonic settings), the greeting of the people and then the collect.

41

Those engaged in the reform sought to make the three most important elements of the introductory rite stand out clearly : the *entrance song*, the *greeting* (reverence of the altar and greeting of the people), and the *prayer* (collect). These remain the three principal features of this part of the Mass. It was intended that the sign of the cross should remain, but in silence so as not to duplicate the greeting; it was intended that either the Kyrie or the Gloria should be said or sung, but not both at the same Mass. As time went on, and the suggested reforms passed through various hands and viewpoints, other things were added—the traditional trinitarian formula was to accompany the sign of the cross at the beginning, the Introit was to be recited if it was not sung, the penitential act was introduced, and both the Kyrie and Gloria were to be retained.

It will be useful to consider here a point which affects the way the whole rite is celebrated : *singing and music*.

There are two things to be borne in mind here : firstly, that from the nature of the rite itself the entrance song is the most important of the singable parts; secondly, that the singing of entrance song, Kyrie and Gloria, should not be such as to overload the rite and make it of disproportionate length in relation to the liturgy of the word. One of the main reasons that both the Kyrie and the Gloria have been retained is to preserve the heritage of Church music which attaches to these texts. But this rich patrimony needs to be used with discretion. Art forms in the liturgy have often shown a centrifugal tendency, developing for their own sake, losing their original function, and tending to obscure the rite whose significance they were originally intended to bring out more fully and effectively. This does not mean that we should plump for banality or a sterile functionism, but it does mean that the way art forms are supplied should help us to be more aware of the liturgy's depth and riches, and enter more profoundly into its spirit and mood.

We shall now treat each part of the introductory rite briefly.

1. PROCESSION AND ENTRANCE SONG

The Mass normally opens with the procession of the priest accompanied by his ministers. It goes without saying that this movement from sacristy to altar should be long enough to merit the name 'procession', but circumstances differ so much that there can be no hard and fast rules in this regard.

Often, the procession will be longer or shorter according to the solemnity of the particular Mass. The celebrant is preceded by those who are to play a particular role in the celebration, particularly the lector, the deacon (either he or a lector can carry in the lectionary), the commentator if there is one, and the servers. The procession can also, when incense is to be used, be led by the thurifer followed by the cross-bearer and servers with lighted torches, if these are desired to give the celebration further solemnity.

The *Entrance Song* accompanies the procession. Its purpose is 'to open the celebration, to encourage the unity of all present, to lead them spiritually into the mystery of a liturgical season or feast being celebrated, and to accompany the procession of the priest and ministers' (GI, 25). This song is important because it can set the tone of the entire celebration. It may be executed either by the choir (or cantor) and people alternately, or by the people or choir alone.

The antiphon and its psalm from the Roman Gradual may be used, or the antiphons and psalms of the Simple Gradual may be used. This Simple Gradual, whose melodic refrains can be repeated over a series of Sundays and thus learnt easily by the people, lends itself to alternate singing between cantor and congregation.

Hymns approved by the Episcopal Conference may be used instead of the Introit antiphon, but these hymns should be chosen because they are suitable for the feast or liturgical season, for this particular celebration and this part of the Mass—not just because they are generally popular.

If there is no Entrance Song, then the Introit antiphon given in the Missal should be said either by the whole congregation, or by some of the congregation, or by the lector. If none of these solutions is possible, it will be read by the priest himself when he has greeted the assembly (GI, 26).

2. VENERATION OF THE ALTAR AND GREETING OF THE PEOPLE

The three traditional gestures of veneration of the altar are maintained : the profound bow (or genuflection, if this is also a gesture of adoration in honour of the Blessed Sacrament present in the sanctuary), the kissing of the altar and, if desired, the incensation. If there is a deacon and sub-deacon present they also kiss the altar (GI, 27).[1]

There are now only two kisses of the altar, namely at the beginning and end of Mass. The altar is a symbol of Christ himself, centre of the church and centre of the eucharistic assembly. It is around this altar-table that the Christian family gathers to celebrate the sacrificial meal of the eucharist. The reverence we show the altar expresses the reverence we have for the saving mystery of Christ in our midst, and this is why, when a bishop enters the cathedral church of his diocese for the first time, his first action is to kiss the main altar. The custom of incensing the altar after kissing it expresses the honour in which it is held, and can help introduce the assembly to an atmosphere of prayer and an awareness of the mysteries which are about to be accomplished.

After the veneration of the altar, the celebrant goes to the seat. 'The seat of a celebrant should illustrate his function of presiding over the assembly and directing its prayer' (GI, 271). The Instruction states that any appearance of its being a throne should be avoided. It suggests that the ideal place is at the centre of the sanctuary against the rear wall, but immediately admits that the structure of the church can make this solution undesirable if it impedes rather than facilitates communication between celebrant and congregation. The best solution will often be to have the seat to the side and slightly forward (cf above, page 24). The seats for the other ministers or servers should be so placed as to make it easy for them to fulfil their tasks easily.

When he reaches the seat, the celebrant makes the sign of the cross, saying the formula which normally accompanies this gesture; the people also sign themselves and reply *Amen*.

The celebrant then greets the congregation. This is an important part of the introductory rites. It is normal in any meeting or reunion to greet those who are assembled there, and the Mass is no exception. But the greeting here is more, it is a recognition

---

[1] Episcopal Conferences may replace the kissing of the altar and the book of the Gospels with a gesture of veneration more suitable to the character or customs of their country (GI, 232).

of the presence of Christ in the assembly, in his Church. As Robert Hovda remarks,

'Our assembly gathers, conscious of the unseen and the transcendent. But with our eyes we see, and what we see should be nothing less important than people. Our brothers and our sisters are the first signs of Christ's presence, and the most important one.'[2]

The way the priest greets the assembly is important :

'Whatever a priest is feeling at the time—whether he is nervous, worried or irritable, his greeting should be warm, confident and friendly, and should establish that rapport between himself and the congregation which is to continue throughout the celebration.'[3]

Besides the customary 'The Lord be with you', and the bishop's 'Peace be with you' which reminds us of our Lord's own greeting to his disciples after his resurrection (Lk 24 :36), a number of alternative greetings, taken from St Paul's Epistles, are given. It is to be hoped that these beautiful greetings will be widely used. Hallowed by centuries of use in the liturgies of the East, they probably had a liturgical origin, e.g. 'the grace of the Lord Jesus Christ, the love of God and the fellowship of the Holy Spirit be with you all' (2 Cor 13 :13).

3. THE 'FEW WORDS'

After the greeting, the celebrant, or a deacon, minister or commentator, may say a few words introducing the faithful into the celebration of the day (GI, 26, 86; cf 68a; OMP, 3).[4] Imaginative use of this brief address can be very helpful in orientating the attention of the congregation, and helping to create a feeling of community among them. It allows the celebrant to fill out the greeting in a more spontaneous and informal way. Note however that the Instruction states emphatically that the words should be *few* in number.

[2] Robert W. Hovda, 'Style and Presence in Celebration', *Worship* 41 (1967), p. 521.
[3] Raymond Clarke, *Sounds Effective,* Geoffrey Chapman, London 1969, p. 66.
[4] OMP, Ordo Missae Cum Populo.

4. THE PENITENTIAL ACT, OR ACT OF PENANCE

It was only after considerable discussion in the Liturgy Consilium that the insertion of a penitential act was accepted. The majority felt that something was necessary to take the place of the *Confiteor,* and that an acknowledgement of our sinfulness before celebrating the eucharist was desirable. In the words of the *Didaché,* 'assembled together on the day of the Lord, break the bread and give thanks, having acknowledged your sins, in order that your sacrifice might be pure'. A penitential act of a similar kind is held in great esteem by many of the other Christian churches.

Once accepted in principle, the question was : where should it go? Of the many suggestions made, two appeared to be practical possibilities : either after the greeting of the people by the priest at the beginning of the Mass, or during the preparation of gifts and united to the kiss of peace. In favour of this last solution were our Lord's words : 'If you are bringing your offering to the altar and there remember that your brother has something against you, leave your offering there before the altar, go and be reconciled with your brother first, and then come back and present your offering' (Mt 5 : 23–24). In this place, it would become an act of reconciliation with God and our brothers before entering into the heart of the eucharistic celebration.

After much debate, it was decided to leave the kiss of peace in its traditional position in the Roman rite, namely, directly linked with communion. As a result, it seemed that the penitential rite, without the kiss of peace, was best placed in the position it now occupies after the initial greetings.

Three forms of the penitential act are offered. In each, the priest invites the community to a spirit of repentence, a reminder of that profound conversion of heart to God which was at the forefront of our Lord's preaching. The invitation is followed by a brief period of silence in which each person becomes aware of himself in the presence of the all-holy God whose love invites us to return to him. Then there is a choice between :

(i)   *Collective act of penance by means of a simplified form of the Confiteor,* followed by the priest's Misereatur. The simplified version of the Confiteor includes an acknowledgement of sin before

God and one another, and does not enumerate individual saints, but having invoked the Virgin Mary, invokes all the angels and saints. The idea of sin by omission—a common enough form of sin after all—has also been inserted.

(ii) *A short dialogue followed by the Misereatur.* Perhaps more could be made of the pause of silence when this form is used.

(iii) *The third form is of a more supplicatory nature.* It combines invocations with the 'Lord, have mercy'. The invocations offered in the Order of the Mass can be substituted by others if desired. Here too the Misereatur of the priest is answered by the people's Amen.

In the April (1968) meeting of the Liturgy Consilium, the question was raised as to what value was to be attributed to the 'pardon, absolution and remission of sins' in the priest's Indulgentiam.[5] In the light of ecumenical theology and changing attitudes to the practice of confession, the point was a delicate one. The Indulgentiam formula was accordingly dropped from the Mass text and reserved to the Sacrament of Penance itself, thus making clear that the penitential rite was not intended to include strictly sacramental absolution.

5. KYRIE, OR LORD HAVE MERCY

Next, if the Kyrie has not been included in the penitential act (as it is in the third penitential form), it is sung or said. The Kyrie had its origins in an ancient litany form, and is not only a supplication for God's mercy but also an acclamation in acknowledgement of God. It is normally said or sung by all, the people alternating with choir or cantor. The General Instruction says that although each of the acclamations will now be said or sung twice only, for musical or pastoral reasons the acclamations may be repeated more than twice, or a *brief* 'trope' inserted. This word 'trope' refers to amplifications in verse form accompanying the Kyrie. A whole literature of these 'Kyrie tropes' developed in the later Middle Ages, but they gradually developed to such proportions that they were completely out of place in this part of the Mass. In his reform of the Missal in 1570, Pius V cut them away and thus brought back a better balance. The long and complex polyphonic settings which later accompanied the

[5] Cf Adalberto Mª Franquesa, *op. cit.*, p. 233.

Kyrie tended to undo his work. If history is not to repeat itself, composers should be encouraged to make the settings to the Kyrie simple and reasonably brief.

6. GLORIA, OR GLORY TO GOD

'The Gloria is that very ancient and venerable hymn by which the Church, assembled in the Holy Spirit, glorifies and prays to God the Father and the Lamb. It is sung either by the assembly of the faithful, or by the people alternately with the choir, or by the choir. If it is not sung, it is to be said either all together or by alternation.

'It is sung or said on Sundays outside the times of Advent and Lent, as also on solemnities and feasts, and in particularly solemn celebrations' (GI, 31).

The hymn is therefore not said on ferial days of Christmas and paschal time, nor on memorial days of the saints. The 'particularly solemn celebrations' mentioned here do not depend on the calendar but on local circumstances and reasons for celebration.

Since this is the first time that we meet the terminology of the new calendar, a few remarks would be in order.

Solemnities: These are the most important days of the liturgical year, and they begin with First Vespers of the preceding day. Some of them also have their own vigil. The principal solemnities are Easter and Christmas, which are both accompanied by a following octave. They are generally equivalent to what the previous calendar called feasts of the first class.

Feasts: These are equivalent to the former feasts of second class. They do not have a first vespers except when it is a question of feasts of the Lord where these occur on Sundays 'per annum'.

Memorials: These can be obligatory or optional. The way in which they integrate with the ferial celebrations is described in the Special Norms accompanying the new calendar.

7. THE PRAYER OR COLLECT

'The priest then invites the people to pray. All remain in silence with the priest for a while, in order that they might be conscious of being in God's presence and express their own prayers interiorly. The priest then proclaims the prayer, which is usually called "the Collect". Through this prayer the nature of the celebration is expressed, and, through the words of the priest, prayer is directed to God the Father, through Jesus Christ, in the Holy Spirit. Uniting themselves with the prayer and giving it their assent, the people make the prayer their own through the acclamation *Amen*' (GI, 32).

The first of the presidential prayers in the Mass, one of the most important elements in the Introductory rites and deeply rooted in the Church's age-old liturgical tradition, this prayer expresses the movement of the entire rite of the Mass and of the whole Christian life: in the Spirit, through Christ, to the Father. Spokesman of the whole assembly, the priest gathers together the prayers of all present (that is why it is called the collect, gathering or collecting all the prayers into one) into the official text of the prayer.

The phrase 'Let us pray' is an invitation to prayer, and is followed by a short period of silence in which the assembly becomes more deeply aware of God's presence. In the new Order of the Mass, this pause of silence is no longer optional but obligatory.

The collect, like the prayer over the gifts and the prayer after communion, is from now on one prayer, and one only (GI, 32). There are no exceptions to this rule. Even prayers formerly linked under one conclusion are no longer permitted. Alone among the three presidential prayers just mentioned, the collect retains the long conclusion which has been customary until now.

With regard to the choice of collect : in all Masses, unless the contrary is stated, the prayer of the Proper is said. In memorial Masses of the Saints' however, the collect is taken either from the Proper or from the Common. On ferial days 'per annum', there is a wide choice : either the collect of the preceding Sunday, or any of the collects from the whole series of thirty-four Sundays, or any of the prayers for particular occasions or needs given in the Missal.

A final remark : these collects are often very concise in their expression, and if they are to be proclaimed intelligibly, they need to be prepared beforehand. The concluding doxology is an integral part of the prayer and therefore should be said with care equal to that required for the rest of the prayer.

CHAPTER IV

The Liturgy of the Word

1. THE LITURGY OF THE WORD IN VATICAN II

One of the most striking features of the Second Vatican Council was the renewed emphasis it laid on sacred scripture. In this it recognized and applauded the renewal in biblical studies over the preceding half century both within and without the Catholic Church. Within the Church, Pius XII's encyclical *Divino Afflante Spiritu* had marked a culminating achievement and a new point of departure. As Cardinal Bea, one of the leaders of the biblical renewal and champion of Christian unity, repeatedly pointed out, the achievements of Vatican II owe a great deal to the work of Pius XII. Perhaps history will give a fairer judgment on the work of this Pope than is often expressed at the present time. It is gradually becoming clear that in many spheres of Church life he was a man remarkably alert to the 'signs of the times' and to the breath of the Spirit among men.

The Council firmly asserted the central importance of the scriptures in the Church's life, and especially in the liturgy where the reading of the scriptures has always found its privileged place.

'Sacred scripture is of paramount importance in the celebration of the liturgy. For it is from scripture that lessons are read and explained in the homily, and psalms are sung; the prayers, collects, and liturgical songs are scriptural in their inspiration, and it is from scripture that actions and signs derive their meaning. Thus if the restoration, progress and adaptation of the sacred liturgy are to be achieved, it is necessary to promote

50

that warm and living love for scripture to which the venerable
tradition of both Eastern and Western rites give testimony'
(*Constitution on the Liturgy,* art. 24).

In explaining why we should have this love for the scriptures,
and in presenting their importance in the Christian life, there is
the profound and beautiful statement of *The Constitution on
Divine Revelation* :

'For in the sacred books, the Father who is in heaven meets
his children with great love and speaks with them; and the
force and power in the word of God is so great that it remains
the support and energy of the Church, the strength of faith for
her sons, the food of the soul, the pure and perennial source of
spiritual life' (art. 21).

For too long the Liturgy of the Word had been considered as
a secondary element in the Mass, and in the reform this situation
had to be righted. *The Constitution on the Liturgy* laid down
the guidelines :

'That the intimate connection between words and rites may
be apparent in the liturgy : in sacred celebrations there is to
be more reading from holy scripture and it is to be more varied
and suitable' (art. 35).

It goes on :

'The treasures of the Bible are to be opened up more lavishly,
so that richer fare may be provided for the faithful at the
table of God's word. In this way, a more representative portion
of the holy scriptures will be read to the people over a set cycle
of years' (art. 51).

This is the conciliar backing for the reform which we shall be
examining, but first of all let us look more closely at the Word of
God itself.

2. THE WORD OF GOD

God, as Louis Bouyer remarks, is not a theology professor.
Just as the first experience of the human word is that of someone
else entering into our life, so too man's experience of God's word

was that of a direct intervention in his life.[1] The Jews, to whom God revealed himself, did not view God's word as a series of messages with concepts to be analysed, parcelled and pigeon-holed. He did not see it this way because he did not experience it in this way. He experienced God's word as God himself, a person, intervening in history. He knew God's word as an event which affected him directly, so directly that it coloured and trans-formed his whole life. It was a deciding reality he could not ignore. In the famous words of Isaiah :

> 'As the rain and the snow come down from the heavens and do not return without watering the earth, making it yield and giving growth to provide seed for the sower and bread for the eating, so the word that goes forth from my mouth does not return to me empty without carrying out my will and suc-ceeding in what it was sent to do' (Is 55 : 10–11).

> 'For Israel, not only is the divine word, like every word worthy of the name, an action, a personal intervention, a presence which asserts and imposes itself, but since it is the word of the Almighty, it produces what it proclaims by its own power. God is "true" not only in the sense that he never lies, but in the sense that what he says is the source of all reality. It is enough that he says it for it to be done.'[2]

It was through the events of history that God revealed himself and the Jews came to know him. This revelation was a progressive one, events gradually unfolding God's plan for mankind—salva-tion history as we call it. But as Bernard Cooke has pointed out, this was not so much a series of events as *an event*.[3] The event referred to is the corporate reality of God's own people, Israel, the vehicle chosen by God in his self-revelation to man :

> 'The important aspect of the life and history of Israel is not that which is historically observable, but rather it is the inner

---

[1] Louis Bouyer, *Eucharist,* University of Notre Dame Press Indiana, 1968, p. 32.

[2] *Ibid.,* p. 33.

[3] Bernard Cooke, 'Word of God : Scripture and Sacrament', a paper from the proceedings of the Society of Catholic College Teachers of Sacred Doc-trine, 1964, and reprinted in the Clergy Study Days of the Chicago Arch-diocesan Liturgy Training Program.

reality of Israel's faith. God's great action on Israel's behalf was the awakening and guiding and nourishing of Israel's life of faith.'[4]

The key event in this faith life was the event by which Israel actually became God's people through its liberation from Egypt and solemn acceptance of the covenant with God at Sinai. Later events were understood in the light of this and judged in relation to it, and accordingly Israel's awareness of its own identity and mission progressively increased. This central event was celebrated in the liturgy, and the oral traditions by which it was carried on and explained from generation to generation gradually took written form in order to ensure their permanence and value. So a good part, even if by no means all, of the Old Testament had a liturgical origin. Naturally enough, these liturgical writings were coloured and interpreted according to the historical circumstances in which the writer found himself, and this brought further understanding of the continuing significance of the events to which they referred.

What place this written word, the scriptures, held in the faith-life of Israel can be seen from the solemn renewals of the covenant described in the Old Testament :

'When King Josiah recalled Israel from its pagan ways in the seventh century B.C., and pledged the nation again to the covenant of Moses, the ceremony began with a public reading of the word of God as contained in the "Book of the Covenant". And only when the people had joined in the covenant in this way was the Passover celebrated again to seal it' (2 Kg 23 : 1–3; 21–24).[5]

The same pattern was followed by Ezra after the Babylonian captivity (Nehemiah, ch. 8) :

'Since it was the word which had formed the people in the first instance, they turned to the word to re-form them and make them more and more truly the People of God.'[6]

---

[4] *Idem.*
[5] Hubert J. Richards, 'God's Word in the Liturgy', in James Crichton (ed.) *The Mass and the People of God,* Burns and Oates, London, 1966, p. 76.
[6] *Ibid.,* p. 77.

Just as, when the scriptures were written, the historical circumstances of the writer brought a deepening interpretation of the original event, so too the situation and events in which the listeners found themselves when the scriptures were read brought a fuller understanding of their content. If this was true in Judaism before the coming of Christ, it was above all true of the time when the 'Word was made flesh'. As St Matthew's Gospel never tires of pointing out, in Christ the scriptures were fulfilled. In Christ man was offered the new covenant, and the eucharist was the sacrament of this covenant. It was natural that when the early Christians gathered to celebrate the eucharist in memory of Christ, the events of our Lord's life and their meaning and significance for those present at the celebration would be recounted and explained. This was primarily the office of the apostles and of those they chose to assist them.

But the apostles were not immortal, and it was necessary that their witness be faithfully recorded and preserved if the Christian faith and tradition were to be handed on unsullied. The witness of the apostles played a key role in the process by which the inspired writers set down their understanding of Christ's life, death and rising to life again. It was the apostles' testimony, as eye-witnesses, that guaranteed the value of the New Testament writings, since they were the vital link of the Church with Christ. The whole of the Church's sacramental life was, and has continued to be, inseparably bound up with the element of apostolicity in the Church.

With the passing of the apostles from the scene, the role of the scriptures in the celebration of the liturgy was at least in part to ensure the continuity in faith between the celebrating community and the apostolic community. It should be noted that among the objects of this faith, the explanation of the eucharist itself held a most important place. The New Testament books themselves amply demonstrate this.[7] Proclaimed in the midst of the eucharistic assembly, the scriptures, both Old and New, re-evoked the faith of the community, prepared the people for the celebration of the eucharist and clarified its significance. Perhaps we should examine this 'clarification' a little further.

The reading of the scriptures is so linked with the celebration of the eucharist that without it the celebration is not fully

[7] Bernard Cooke, op. cit.

intelligible. The sign of the eucharist is only intelligible if we have some understanding of what Christ said and did, and the privileged expression of this understanding is the word of God itself. This word which had a living and spoken origin is destined to have a living and spoken expression : its proclamation in the liturgy. This word *is* living, because in a way that completely surpasses God's presence through his word in the Old Testament Christ is present and active. 'The words I have spoken to you are Spirit and life' (Jn 6 :64). This is just as true of our own generation as it was of those to whom our Lord was speaking. Just as the Lord 'opened the heart of Lydia to accept what Paul was saying' (Acts 16 :14), so too with the word proclaimed in the Church's liturgy today : it is accompanied by the power of Christ's spirit. As *The Constitution on the Liturgy* says : 'Christ is present in his word, since it is he himself who speaks when the holy scriptures are read in the Church' (art. 7).

God's word is always a saving word for those whose hearts are open to receive it, because as we have seen God's word is efficacious : it achieves what it proclaims. The link between word and sacrament follows from this. What is proclaimed in the word, is achieved in the sacrament. The salvation and new life which is announced in the reading of the scriptures, is salvation here and now for those who respond to God's word through communion in Christ's saving event. This communion already begins in the liturgy in listening to the word but culminates in eucharistic communion. Whole-hearted acceptance of God's word inevitably leads the Christian to receive the 'Word made flesh', and so to live by his spirit.

We can see then why the Eucharistic Instruction of 1967 so firmly emphasized the bonds between the two major parts of the Mass :

'Pastors should carefully teach the faithful to participate in the whole Mass showing the close connection between the liturgy of the word and the celebration of the Lord's Supper so that they can see clearly how the two constitute a single act of worship, for the preaching of the word is necessary for the very administration of the sacraments inasmuch as they are sacraments of faith which is born of the word and fed by it. This is especially true of the celebration of Mass, in which it is the purpose of the liturgy of the word to develop the close connection between preaching and hearing the word of God and the eucharistic mystery.

'When, therefore, the faithful hear the word of God they should realize that the wonders it proclaims culminate in the paschal mystery whose memorial is sacramentally celebrated in the Mass. In this way the faithful will be nourished by the word of God which they have received and in a spirit of thanksgiving they will be led on to a fruitful participation in the mysteries of salvation. Thus the Church is nourished by the bread of life which she finds at the table, both of the word of God and of the Body of Christ' (art. 10).

3. THE CHURCH'S TRADITION

'The fundamental connection between the eucharist and the proclamation of the word of God seems to have been perceived from the first by the Christian community.'[8]

In the Acts of the Apostles the early Christian community is described as coming together for the 'teaching of the apostles and the breaking of bread' (Acts 2 :42). Similarly, in one of the earliest descriptions of the Christian eucharist that we possess—that of Justin the Martyr around the middle of the second century—we find the same coupling of both parts of the liturgy :

'On the day which is called Sun-Day, all, whether they live in the town or in the country, gather in the same place.

'Then the memoirs of the Apostles or the writings of the Prophets are read for as long as time allows.

'When the reader has finished the president speaks, exhorting us to live by these noble teachings.

'Then we rise altogether and pray.

'Then as we said earlier, when the prayer is finished bread, wine and water are brought. The president then prays and gives thanks as well as he can and all the people reply with the acclamation "Amen". After this the eucharists are distributed and shared out to everyone and the deacons are sent to take them to those who are absent.'[9]

[8] Joseph Lécuyer, *Le Sacrifice de la Nouvelle Alliance*, 1961, p. 229.

[9] Quoted from Lucien Deiss, *Early Sources of the Liturgy*, Geoffrey Chapman, London, 1967, pp. 25–6.

In the following centuries the structure of the liturgy of the *c)*
word gradually developed, but there was considerable variety in
the number and selection of the readings in the different local
churches. The number of readings varied from two to four, and
on a number of occasions were even more. There were readings
from the Old and New Testament, and the readings were normally part of a *lectio continua* or continuous reading from the
same book. This continuity was broken into as the years went *a)*
on by the development of the different parts of the liturgical year.
In the Roman Rite the relating of the readings to the various
station-churches and saints-days also cut across the principle of
continuity. By the time the readings for the various Sundays of
the year fell into a stable pattern, the resulting lectionary was
rather haphazard and without any consistent underlying pattern.
The choice of readings for such seasons of the Church's year
as Advent and Eastertide was often excellent, but in the Sundays
after Pentecost there was neither rhyme nor reason in the selection   *N. B.*
of readings, and there were considerable sections of the Gospels,
for example, which did not appear at all.

4.   THE NEW LECTIONARY

It is against this background that the lectionary has been
revised, and we shall now attempt to describe its preparation,
structure and content.[10]
                                                a) . PREPARATION
The work involved in the preparation of the lectionary has
been systematic and arduous. The commission within the Liturgy
Consilium, made up of scholars of international repute, began
its work in 1964 by establishing and studying the biblical readings   *i)*
of the Latin liturgies from the sixth to the twelfth centuries,
surveying the readings used by fifteen Oriental rites, and analys-
ing the lectionaries used by the separated Christian churches from
the time of the Protestant Reformation up to the present day.
In this they drew largely on the research carried out over the
preceding fifty years. This was certainly a guarantee that 'a
sound tradition should be retained', which left 'the way open for

---

[10] The presentation given here of the background to the new lectionary
is closely linked with the *Commentarium ad Ordinem lectionum Missae*,
prepared by Gaston Fontaine, Secretary of the Commission for the new
lectionary, and sent by the Congregation for Divine Worship to the Presidents
of Episcopal Conferences and Presidents of National Liturgical Commissions.

legitimate progress', and that 'new forms should in some way grow organically from forms already existing' (*Constitution on the Liturgy*, art. 23).

The work of the exegetes then followed. These men were chosen as experts in particular sections of scripture. They determined texts of major importance for the economy of salvation and, at the same time, easily understandable by the faithful. Their work was passed on to more than a hundred consultors engaged in catechesis and pastoral work. The results of all this were then gradually drawn into shape by the lectionary commission itself, and the finished product was sent out in July 1967 to all the Episcopal Conferences. The heads of national liturgical commissions were invited to name consultors—exegetes, pastors, teachers, etc.—to give their comments on the proposed lectionary.

It was on the basis of the replies received from around eight hundred persons, groups or institutes that the first projected lectionary was revised. It was a complete revision and very considerable changes were made in the light of the criticisms. The final revisions of major importance were approved by the plenary meeting of the Consilium in April 1968, and in the following months the final work was carried out on the Sanctoral Cycle and Masses for Particular Occasions.

Bearing the date of 25 May 1969, the new lectionary actually made its appearance in August of that year. It is divided into six main sections:

(i) *The Temporal Cycle*, with two sections: the Sundays and feasts on the one hand, the weekdays or ferias on the other.

(ii) *The Proper of the Saints*, in accordance with the new calendar of the Church's year. Unlike former missals, this now follows the development of the civil year, from 1 January to 31 December.

(iii) *The Commons*, for the dedication of churches and for saints-days: the Blessed Virgin Mary, martyrs, pastors, doctors of the Church, virgins and a general category for all the other saints. Thus the former title of 'non-virgin' saints has disappeared.

(iv) Under the general title of *Ritual Masses*, there are readings put forward for the catechumenate rites and for adult baptism, infant baptism, admission of validly baptized persons into full communion with the Church, confirmation, first communion, ordinations, marriages, blessings of abbots and abbesses, consecration of virgins and religious profession and finally funerals and Masses for the dead.

(v) Twenty formularies for *Masses for Various Occasions,* corresponding in general terms to the former Votive Masses. They are now divided into four sections in accordance with the intention of the prayers of the faithful : the Church, public intentions, varying circumstances of general concern or interest, some particular needs.

(vi) Retaining the title of *Votive Masses,* eight formularies for Masses in honour of the Blessed Trinity, the Cross of Christ, the Blessed Sacrament, the Sacred Heart, the Precious Blood, the Holy Name of Jesus, the Holy Spirit, the Apostles.

(i) *The Sunday and Feast-day Lectionary*

This is undoubtedly the most important section of the new lectionary, since it is this that the majority of the Christian people are going to hear. It is through these readings that they can attain a fuller understanding of the mystery of salvation and thus allow it to enter more fully into their lives. It will be helpful to consider the structure of the lectionary and the principles upon which it is based.

a) *Three year cycle and three readings:* The Council had insisted that a wider variety and greater number of readings should be offered 'over a set cycle of years'. It did not indicate any exact number. After considerable study and discussion a three year cycle of readings was chosen as being preferable to either a two year or a four year cycle. It afforded ample presentation of the scriptures, without leading to repetitions, and meant that a year could be assigned to each of the Synoptic Gospels.

To determine the present year of the cycle a simple means, easy to remember, was chosen. Of the three years, A, B and C, the year C is that which is divisible by 3 (it is sufficient to add the figures together to see whether the total is a multiple of 3). Thus the years 1968, 1971 and 1974 are C years. The years will follow are A years : 1969, 1972 and 1975. The years which precede are B years : 1967, 1970 and 1973. It is intended that the liturgical year beginning with the first Sunday of Advent carries the date of the civil year beginning with the following

1 January. The lectionary thus came into force on 30 November 1969, and the readings for that year are taken from the B cycle since 1970 is a B year.[11]

On each Sunday or major feast day three readings are offered in the following order : Old Testament (replaced by the Acts of the Apostles in Paschal time), the writings of the Apostles (Epistles or Book of Revelation), Gospel. There are many precedents for this in the Church's tradition and it was a feature of the Roman Rite, among others. This scheme of three readings puts the unity between the two Testaments in clear relief and shows the continuity of salvation history; begun and proclaimed in the Old Testament, it attains its full realization in the paschal mystery of Christ and it is through the apostolic preaching that it reaches all generations. It will be of great assistance to the priest in his preaching, and it was the view of the commission working on the lectionary that it is practically the only way of having all the faithful hear a number of Old Testament texts which are practically unknown to the majority.

Questions arise here which cannot be passed over in silence. How much of the Old Testament should be read in our churches today? What do the scriptures mean to men of our day? Adequate answers to these questions would take us into the whole question of the relevance of Christianity and into the secularization debate, but here we can only make a few observations.

Firstly, the inspired word of God has a perennial value which nothing can dim :

> 'The holy scriptures—from these you can learn the wisdom that leads to salvation through faith in Jesus Christ. All scripture is inspired by God and can profitably be used for teaching, for refuting error, for guiding people's lives and teaching them to be holy' (2 Tim 3 : 15–16).

As we are all aware from our own experience this does not mean that all parts of the scriptures are equal in value, or that all of them are immediately suitable for reading to a normal Sunday congregation. Discretion and selectivity are necessary. But the Church has never hesitated to read considerable sections of the Old Testament at the Sunday celebration. The under-

---

[11] In the *Lectionary,* published by Geoffrey Chapman, London, 1969, years A, B and C are called years 1, 2 and 3.

standing of Christianity as a religion founded on the actions of
God in human history, rather than on the speculations of theo-
logians or philosophers, can only be achieved through having
some knowledge of the events, recounted in the Old Testament,
which culminated in the coming of Christ. Any presentation of
the Church and her sacramental life today will require some
awareness of how God's plan of salvation has gradually worked
out in history both before and after Christ, and to understand
God's action in the past will help in the understanding of his
action today.

The Old Testament not only throws light on the New Testament, 'today the scripture has been fulfilled in your hearing'
Luke 4 :21), it has a great deal which in itself is of perennial
religious value. The difficulty remains that many of the ideas
are couched in language and imagery which originate in a
culture very different from our own. To what extent then should
people be 'educated in biblical categories' and to what extent
should biblical categories be broken down and expressed in contemporary imagery and thought-patterns? It is a two-way process,
and it would seem that both must be attempted. Some awareness
of the major Bible themes would seem a necessary element in our
self-awareness and identity as Christians. Insight into the way
God's word has become incarnate in the past takes us part way to
perceiving the way God is active in our world in our time.

The extent to which the great majority of Christians can be
educated in the mentality of the scriptures is limited. The degree
to which such an education is desirable is also limited.

> 'One is tempted to see here a parallel with the judaizing
> problem that so vexed the early Church—must the prospective
> Christian accept the law of Moses, in effect become a Jew,
> before he could become a Christian? The early Church's
> answer to this, after some initial hesitation, was a fairly strong
> negative. But are we in some sense asking people to become
> first century Christians, so that they can become more fully
> Christians of the twentieth century?'[12]

As we said above, it is a two-way process. Whatever we present
through the scriptures must be understood in terms of a person's

[12] Brendan Byrne, 'The Scripture Readings at Mass : Are they really
Communicating', *Worship*, 43 (March 1969) p. 169.

experience of life and self-experience. This will involve the re-interpretation of the scriptures, their application, in terms of the contemporary understanding and situation of those who are hearing God's word. This task does not belong exclusively to the liturgy, but extends to the whole field of Christian teaching and education. In the liturgy, the privileged place for this linking of scripture with life is the homily. The other parts of the Mass, the prayers and songs, should also help in this linking of scripture and life. It may be that short introductions to the readings, read by a commentator for example, could be very helpful in clarifying the understanding of the scriptures which are to be read, and offer a good basis for the homily, but if the first half of the Mass is not to be hopelessly overloaded, the emphasis will have to be on *short* introductions.

This last remark draws our attention to the length of the readings themselves. The aim in the revision has been that they should be neither too short nor too long. If the reading is too short it is unable to engage the listener's attention; if the reading is too long it can become wearisome and fail to sustain the listener's interest. An important distinction was also made: narrative texts must be allowed space to develop and normally hold the listener's attention easily, while texts which are primarily doctrinal in character tend to be highly condensed and concise and should normally be short. For this reason, readings from the Epistles are normally short. Lest the liturgy of the word should become too long with three readings, the aim has generally been to keep them of moderate and roughly equal length. For some occasions the lectionary offers a choice between a longer and a shorter reading. Good examples are the Gospels of the 3rd, 4th and 5th Sundays of Lent—these are the famous Johannine texts of the Samaritan woman, the man born blind and the raising of Lazarus. The choice between longer and shorter form allows for adaptation to the concrete possibilities of time, spiritual preparation and powers of assimilation of the assembly.

Referring to the three scripture readings, the General Instruction states:

'In this way the Christian people are taught the continuity of the work of salvation in accordance with God's wonderful plan. It is therefore highly desirable that these three readings should be effectively proclaimed. However, for pastoral reasons and by decree of the Episcopal Conference, the use of only two readings is permitted in certain places' (GI, 318).

This does not mean that three readings, when proferred by the lectionary, can be forbidden—such a ruling would be completely contrary to the intentions of the legislator. What is intended is that it should not always be obligatory to have three readings, unless the local hierarchy decrees otherwise. Already a disputed point within the Liturgy Consilium, the bishops of the Synod were in favour of keeping this option open. It was felt that sometimes, particularly when there is little or no opportunity to present and explain the readings, three readings might be too much. While this is so, the preference remains clearly in favour of the three readings.

But what of the situation where there are to be only two readings on a Sunday? Which of the first two is to be preferred? Above all it should be remembered that 'it must not be just a question of which is the easiest or shortest reading' (GI, 318). As the introduction to the lectionary itself states (no. 8A), those texts should be chosen which best convey an understanding of the mystery of salvation. The choice will normally fall on those which best harmonize with the Gospel, with the liturgical season or feast, or which are best suited to the particular congregation present. One should be careful of omitting the readings taken from the more important books of the scriptures. During Lent, for example, the Old Testament texts presenting the great landmarks of salvation history—from creation to the time of the Kings in Israel—should not be overlooked. On the Sundays 'per annum', after Epiphany and Pentecost, the semi-continuous reading of the Epistles should be safeguarded. One thing that should be avoided as far as possible is chopping and changing from Old Testament to New Testament on alternate Sundays. That would only cause confusion and cut across the whole lay-out of the lectionary.

b) *Harmonization or continuous reading?* The choice between the first two texts on those Sundays or in those Masses when three readings have not been preferred, is closely connected with the two principles on which the texts of the lectionary are based : the principle of the harmonization of the readings between themselves, and the principle of 'continuity' within the same book of scripture so that the internal development of its thought and content may be followed through and assimilated. The balancing of these two principles was one of the most difficult problems facing those working on the lectionary, since, while much can be said in favour of both principles, they are not easily reconciled.

The harmonization of the readings around a single theme or event has many pastoral advantages and has always been found, at least on major feasts, in all the liturgies of the Church. This tradition has been maintained in the new lectionary for major feasts and liturgical seasons. This facilitates both the preparation of the homily by the celebrant and the assimilation of the key ideas of day or season by the faithful. Members and consultors of the Consilium were unanimous, however, in rejecting proposals that the readings of each Sunday should always relate to a single theme or that the readings should always harmonize with one another. To do this would be to impose our own intellectual preoccupations and *a priori* schemes on the scriptures, completely oblivious to the inspired writer's exposition of his thought or narrative.

Where there is harmonization, it is normally between the Old Testament and the Gospel. It is not a question of artificial links, based for instance on the presence of a word or proper name which is of secondary importance in the text itself. In a number of cases, emphasis has been given to implicit or explicit quotations which create a genuine internal cohesion between the texts. In any case the texts from Old Testament and Gospels clarify one another, and this makes it easier to grasp the unity of the whole economy of salvation. The *titles of the readings* are very important for this reason : using the words of the texts themselves they show the link between them. A typical example is the Third Sunday of Advent. In the A cycle we find the first reading from Isaiah with the title 'God himself will come and save us' and the Gospel from Matthew with the title : 'Are you the one who is to come, or have we to wait for someone else?' If there is to be a very brief comment before the reading, these titles will often be useful in helping to lead people to the heart of the reading.

Outside the main seasons of the Church's year, semi-continuous reading of the Epistles and Gospels has been adopted, but the readings are in two completely independent lists and do not harmonize with one another—except insofar as all the New Testament harmonizes in Christ! Even in the Roman Missal as we have had it in recent years, there are vestiges of semi-continuous readings of this kind, e.g. the readings from John's Gospel in the second half of Lent and several of the Pauline Epistles on the Sundays after Pentecost. In the three year cycle, one of the synoptic Gospels is assigned to each year. In year A there is Matthew, year B is Mark and year C is Luke. This pattern is not over-rigid : John's Gospel is used particularly at Christmas, in Lent and at Easter, and chapter 6 of that Gospel takes up 5 Sundays of year B thus making up for the brevity of Mark.

With regard to the Epistles, in year A there are the first four chapters of the first letter to the Corinthians (7 Sundays), the letters to the Romans (16 Sundays) and Philippians (4 Sundays) and the first letter to the Thessalonians (5 Sundays). In year B there are chapters 6 to 11 of the first letter to the Corinthians (5 Sundays), the second letter to the Corinthians (8 Sundays), the letter to the Ephesians (7 Sundays), the letter of James (5 Sundays) and chapters 2 to 10 of the letter to the Hebrews (7 Sundays). Year C opens with chapters 12 to 15 of the first letter to the Corinthians (7 Sundays) and then come the letter to the Galatians (6 Sundays), Colossians (4 Sundays), chapters 11–12 of the letter to the Hebrews (4 Sundays), the letter to Philemon (1 Sunday), the first letter to Timothy (3 Sundays), the second letter to Timothy (4 Sundays) and the second letter to the Thessalonians (3 Sundays). The first letter to the Corinthians is spread over three years because of its length, but also because the way it deals with many diverse subjects lends itself to this solution. Hebrews is not the easiest of the Epistles, and for this reason it is spread over two years instead of eleven consecutive Sundays.

The readings are 'semi-continuous'. On the one hand it was not possible to read the whole of the New Testament on Sundays, and on the other hand there are a good number of texts which are either particularly difficult to understand or of secondary interest. Choice has been made, both in the Epistles and the Gospels, of the more important readings which the Christian people should hear at least once in three years.

Another point which was considered when choosing the readings for particular Sundays, was the traditional usage in the Church of particular books during certain periods of the Church's year. We have already seen the use of John's Gospel in Lent and Eastertide. The 'spiritual' Gospel, as it was called, it is the Gospel which gives the deepest insight into the mystery of Christ loving his own even to the end, and his glorification in the 'hour' determined by his Father.

The use of Isaiah during Advent and Christmas is likewise traditional. By its analogy with the persecuted Christ, the book of Jeremiah is well placed in the context of the end of Lent and beginning of Holy Week. The Acts of the Apostles has been used after Easter by almost all the rites of the Church. In the new lectionary the Acts are used in place of the Old Testament in the first reading. This underlines the nature of Easter-Pentecost as the source of the Church's life. The Acts present the early days of the Church lived in the life-giving presence of the Spirit of the risen Christ. In year A of the period after Easter the first letter of Peter is used for the second reading. Since much of this letter seems to have originated in instructions regarding the nature of baptism, it is well-fitted for paschal time. In year B, the second reading is taken from St John's first letter, and year C is from the Apocalypse. These two also tie in well with paschal time. In the first the Apostle 'shows how we as children of God must necessarily live the life of integrity which, for John, is the only thing which fulfils the twin commandments: faith in Jesus Christ, the son of God, and love of the brethren'.[13] The Apocalypse, or Book of Revelation, shows how in the middle of persecutions the Church lives the life of Christ, victor over death and evil, and looks forward to his return in glory.

(ii) *The Weekday or Ferial Lectionary*

Over the last few years the use of provisional weekday lectionaries has prepared the way for the new weekday lectionary. The experience of its use in many countries and situations was of considerable help to the commission preparing the readings. The weekday lectionary is characterized by three points:

a) *Two readings:* Except for Sundays, solemnities and particular

[13] 'Introduction to St John', *Jerusalem Bible*, Darton Longman Todd, London, 1967, pp. 144-5.

celebrations, there are only two readings. The first is taken from the Old or the New Testaments, while the second is always the Gospel. Since the Ember Days have disappeared from the Temporal Cycle and their celebration is left to the decision of Episcopal Conferences under the form of Masses for Special Needs, there are no longer any Masses which possess more than two readings except for Ash Wednesday.

b) *Cycle of one or two years:* For the major seasons of the liturgical year (Advent, Christmas, Lent and Paschal time), there is only one annual cycle for the two readings. On the ferias outside the seasons of the year, the same readings from the Gospel are read each year while the first reading is spread over a two year cycle. This means that a greater number of texts can be read, and ensures a more complete presentation of the principal books of the Old and of the New Testament.

c) *Semi-continuous reading or harmonization:* Completely independent of the Sunday lectionary, the weekday lectionary is largely based on the principle of semi-continuous reading of the books that make up the scriptures. The most important of these are very much in evidence. From the other books passages of special interest are read. Some of the passages already read on the Sundays are taken up again in the continuous weekly reading (the Gospels above all) in order to safeguard the literary and spiritual unity of the book being read. During Advent and Lent the readings of the Old Testament and Gospels are normally harmonized, either strictly or by presenting one or other of the traditional themes of these readings. At Christmas and Easter the two readings develop in independent series.

Choice of readings?

'In the ferial lectionary readings are proposed for each day of the week throughout the course of the year. Normally these readings are used on the days to which they are assigned, unless a solemnity or feast occurs. If, however, the continuous reading is broken on account of a feast or particular celebration, the priest is permitted to choose either to link up the omitted texts with the other readings or to decide which texts it is preferable to read' (GI, 319).

This freedom of choice obviously presupposes that at the beginning of the week one works out what feasts or celebrations will occur over the coming days, and carefully choose the readings so as to help the congregation.

To give an example : from 17 to 24 December, strictly continuous readings from the Gospels of Matthew and Luke present the sequence of events leading up to the birth of Jesus. The fourth Sunday of Advent will fall on one of these days, thus breaking the continuity of the reading. It will be necessary to work out how the readings are to be linked or to choose the more important of the series.

When celebrating with particular groups there is further choice :

'In Masses for particular groups, the priest may select readings from those occurring in that particular week which are best suited to the group for which he is celebrating' (GI, 319).

And in the Instruction of the Congregation for Divine Worship, 15 May 1969, regarding the celebration of Mass for particular groups, this permission was enlarged : 'In the liturgy of the word, readings adapted to the particular celebration can be chosen from approved lectionaries.' (This appears to be the only point where this Instruction of 15 May extends present legislation regarding the celebration of the eucharist. It merely repeats the stipulation of can. 822 requiring the approval of the local Ordinary for celebrations of Mass outside a church or oratory, but also refers to no. 7 of the Motu Proprio *Pastorale Munus* where is it said that the residential bishop, or those to whom he has delegated this faculty, may, for a sufficiently serious reason, grant this faculty habitually.)

(iii) *The Lectionary for the Sanctoral Cycle*

Two series of readings are put forward in this section.

a) *Proper of the Saints:* Under the traditional title 'Proper of the Saints', there is a section which follows the new calendar and offers a selection of proper texts and of texts taken from the 'Commons' of the saints. The solemnities have three readings, while the feasts and memorials have only two. The solemnities and feasts have proper texts, and the reading of these is obligatory. For the memorial-days of the saints, obligatory or not, the lectionary sometimes gives texts which are proper in the strict sense—these are readings which treat expressly of the saint being commemorated and such readings are obligatory : for example, on 26 January for saints Timothy and Titus, on 22 August for St Mary Magdalen, on 29 August for St Martha. Normally the lectionary offers 'appropriated' readings, referring you to a Common, or even several Commons : as when for instance a saint is at the same time a bishop and martyr.

Often enough this or that text, whether or not it is taken from the Commons, is suggested for use in a commemoration if it corresponds better to the gifts with which the Spirit endowed a particular saint or indicates the importance the person has had in the life of the Church. These texts are in no sense obligatory. Where a saint is particularly venerated and loved their use will often be welcomed, but the continuity of the weekday readings is also a value to be safeguarded.

b) *Commons of the Saints:* The other section gives the Commons of the Saints. There has been a simplification in the distribution and grouping of the former Roman Missal.

Here is a list of the new Commons : Dedication of a church, the Blessed Virgin Mary, martyrs, pastors, doctors of the Church, virgins, and the general category of 'saints' for those who do not come into the previous categories.

Each category gives a fairly abundant choice of readings from both Old and New Testaments, some being intended specifically for paschal time. For the last group or category there is a wide variety of texts on sanctity in general (61 in all). Some passages are especially applicable to those who have exercised works of mercy or have educated youth. Similarly, in the Common of Pastors, some texts are indicated which are particularly well suited for feasts of canonized popes.

The introduction to the lectionary makes it clear that one can always draw on the texts of the category of saints in general, whatever the memorial being celebrated, provided it does not have readings which are strictly proper to it. This is further proof of how the choice of texts has widened.

The Commons give lists for three possible readings. These three readings are not obligatory unless it is a question of a solemnity : principal patron of the place or of the town, dedication of a church or anniversary of a dedication, titular patron of the church, founder or principal patron of an Order or Congregation.[14]

[14] Cf Normae universales de Anno liturgico et de Calendario, n. 59, para. 1.

(iv) *The Lectionary for Masses for various occasions and needs*

The last part of the lectionary covers what the General Instruction describes as 'Missae ad diversa', and of which it gives three kinds:

a) 'Ritual Masses, in which certain sacraments, sacramentals or their anniversary commemoration are celebrated'; this refers to baptism, marriages, funerals, etc.

b) 'Masses for various needs which are celebrated in particular circumstances, whether they are occasional or regularly occurring'; examples are Masses for Christian unity, for Christians under persecution, for peace and justice, for the beginning of the civil year, etc.

c) 'Votive Masses, freely chosen in the interests of the piety of the faithful, regarding the mysteries of the Lord or in honour of the Blessed Virgin Mary and the saints'; examples are votive Masses of the Sacred Heart, of the Holy Spirit, of the Holy Cross. Again, a wide selection of readings is offered.

5. THE SONGS OR CHANTS IN THE LITURGY OF THE WORD: THE RESPONSORIAL PSALM AND THE SONG BEFORE THE GOSPEL

In the minds of those preparing the new lectionary, this part of the liturgy of the word was not a secondary thing but something of considerable importance. In the Music Instruction of 1967 we find the statement:

> 'The song after the ʿ...ɔns, be it in the form of gradual or responsorial psalm, haʾ a special importance among the songs of the Proper. By its very nature, it forms part of the liturgy of the word. It should be performed with all seated and listening to it—and, what is more, participating in it as far as possible' (art. 33).

The General Instruction also refers to the responsorial psalm as 'an integral part of the liturgy of the word' (GI, 36). Yet there are a good many priests who do not share this enthusiasm. If the reading of the Old Testament today is a problem, they say, this is particularly true of a great number of the psalms. Some of the psalms, the objection continues, could never be used for the people and the use of much of the psalter requires a preparation which normal congregations just do not have.

As far as I can see, there is no simple solution to this problem. The scriptures can never be just an optional extra for the Christian, and the psalms are an important part of them. The psalms offer an enormously rich variety of prayers and hymns for personal and collective use, and over the centuries of Christianity men have drawn on the endless resources of the psalter as a source of prayer. There is no reason why this should suddenly cease. But the difference between our industrialized and technological society and the culture and society in which the psalms originated, restricts their use with an 'average' congregation.[15] This is a problem which needs thinking through, and practical experimentation will have to be allowed if the answers are to be forthcoming.

The question arises—especially for children's Masses—as to whether an age in which people are becoming more and more accustomed to the semi-visual presentation of ideas and events does not make demands in the liturgical presentation of the word of God.[16] One thing is clear, we must be selective in the psalms and parts of the psalms that are offered in the course of a normal Mass.

Of all the psalm-elements in the Mass, the responsorial psalm is the most important. Let us look at the form it takes in the new lectionary, and the principles on which selection of the psalms has been made.

(i) *Nature of Responsorial Psalm in the Lectionary*

While the responsorial psalm does have a meditative quality, since it encourages a deeper reflection on God's word, it is essentially a prayer or song of response to the word which has been

---

[15] There are many outstanding books and commentaries on the psalms. Two fairly short and readable books concerned with their relevance for the Christian today are Thomas Worden, *The Psalms are Christian Prayer,* Geoffrey Chapman, London, 1966; *Fifty Psalms,* a new translation with commentaries, Burns Oates, London, 1969.

[16] Ewen Derrick, *Growing in Community*, Geoffrey Chapman, London, 1969, has some interesting points to make on the visual presentation of the word to children at Mass.

proclaimed. Event and historical reality as God's word was, the Jew's response to it was the way he actually lived, the things he in fact did. But just as God communicated himself not only in what he did but also in what he said, so too his people responded both in what they did and in what they said. In the liturgy both God's action and the people's response find ritualized expression, an expression which increases the people's awareness of all God has done and is doing for them, deepens their faith and love for him, and evokes a fuller and more whole-hearted response.

In the Christian liturgy too the proclamation of God's word and the people's response continues. The supreme response to this word is the eucharistic liturgy which follows, but throughout the celebration of Mass, proclamation of God's action amongst us and the expression of man's response continually mingle and overlap. In the responsorial psalm both elements are present, but its aspect of 'community response' to God's word is something which should not be lost sight of in the celebration.

In the new lectionary this part of the Mass is drawn up in the following way : on Sundays and ferias a proper psalm has been assigned to each Mass. Coming after the first reading, it is normally chosen because of its connection with it. The verses are grouped in strophes, normally of equal length, in order to facilitate the singing of the psalm verses by cantors or choir. The response or refrain often indicates the reason why a particular psalm has been chosen, since it is often a verse which expresses the character of the psalm or which best links the psalm with one of the readings. Lucien Deiss,[17] one of those closely involved in preparing this part of the lectionary, has outlined the way the psalms were chosen :

a)   When the first reading or the Epistle quotes a psalm, the lectionary often uses the psalm for the gradual or responsorial psalm. An example is the first Monday of Easter week where the Epistle is taken from the first chapter of the Acts and one of the key quotations is from psalm 16, which is therefore used in the gradual.

b)   When the Gospel quotes a psalm, the lectionary often uses this—by way of an anticipated response—for the gradual.

[17] Lucien Deiss, 'Le Psaume Graduel' in Le Lectionnaire Dominical, no. 3 of the second Assemblées du Seigneur series, Cerf, Paris, 1969, pp. 49–72.

An example is the first Sunday of Lent when the Gospel presentation of the temptation of Christ is connected with psalm 91.

c) The lectionary often selects a psalm because of its literary connections with the first reading. This is not just a question of similar words, but of mood or context, e.g. fourth Sunday of the year in the C cycle where the first chapter of Jeremiah develops the same theme as the first part of psalm 70.

d) Even where there is no literary connection, psalms are sometimes used if they help to throw light on or underline the content or message of the other readings, e.g. 'Good Shepherd' Sunday (fourth after Easter) in year A has psalm 23 'The Lord is my shepherd'.

e) Psalms which in liturgical tradition have been in wide use during the major liturgical seasons, are taken up into the new lectionary, e.g. psalm 72 for Epiphany, psalm 22 for the Passion.

f) Where none of these reasons suggested the use of a psalm, selection was made from psalms otherwise not used which seemed well suited to general use.

Besides the proper psalm and versicle (refrain), the lectionary offers two complementary lists. The first of these provides a (i) number of refrains or responses which could be used during a given liturgical season instead of the 'proper' refrain, while still using the psalm assigned to the day. Like the *Simple Gradual*— already printed and published, which may be used in conjunction with the new lectionary—this has the advantage that people can learn a refrain and use it repeatedly over a number of Sundays, e.g. in Advent, Lent or after Pentecost.[18] The second list presents (ii) a choice of psalms common to a particular liturgical season and capable of replacing the psalms assigned for each Mass.

For solemnities and feasts of the saints, the lectionary also gives a proper psalm and response. For memorial-days of saints the lectionary refers you to the list of Commons. A choice of psalms for Ritual Masses, Votive Masses and Masses for various needs is also offered. The various ways in which the responsorial psalm can be sung or said will be considered later under the title 'Actual celebration of the liturgy of the word' (p. 78).

[18] An English version of *The Simple Gradual*, with musical settings, edited by John Ainslie, is published by Geoffrey Chapman, London, 1969.

(ii) *The song or chant before the Gospel*

The Gospel is normally preceded by another chant or song which does not have a specific name. It is fundamentally an acclamation, a recognition of the presence of Christ in the proclamation of the Gospel. In the ancient liturgies the acclamation—which is normally Alleluia with a versicle—accompanied the solemn procession with the Gospel book. As it stands in the new lectionary, it is normally composed of a double element :

a) Firstly a popular acclamation, which for most of the year is *Alleluia* (meaning 'Praise the Lord'). Coming as it does from psalms which were included in the *hallel,* this acclamation was almost certainly used by Our Lord himself at the Last Supper. It characterizes the Christian's joy at Christ's victory over death and sin, and is therefore especially connected with paschal time.

b) In Lent, the period when the Church prepares to celebrate the new Pasch, other formulae of praise are used. Examples are 'Praise and glory to you, Lord Jesus' or 'Glory to Christ, eternal word of the living God'.

The acclamation, *Alleluia* or otherwise, is accompanied by a second element—a versicle. This versicle is proper for the most important feasts of the liturgical year and certain Sundays, and may be selected from a plentiful choice on the other Sundays, ferias, Commons of the saints, Ritual Masses, Masses for particular needs and Votive Masses. Many of these versicles are taken from the Gospel for which they are designed to prepare the way, e.g. 'This is my Son, the Beloved, listen to him'.

(iii) *The Sequences*

The Sequences are no longer obligatory except on the days of Easter and Pentecost. The lectionary gives the texts of the four sequences which remain in the new Missal : *Victimae paschali laudes, Veni Sancte Spiritus, Lauda Sion* and *Stabat Mater.* In accordance with what was already stated in the *Simple Gradual,* it is permissible to use only the last four strophes of the *Lauda Sion,* i.e. beginning with *Ecce panis Angelorum.* These sequences no longer have *Alleluia* or *Amen* at the end—in order that they may be better integrated with the surrounding texts.

Since people will normally stand to sing the *Alleluia*, or at least to listen to it being sung, just prior to the reading of the Gospel, it is logical to place the sequence before the *Alleluia* is sung. This is in fact what the new lectionary does every time it mentions the sequences.

6. HOMILY, CREED, PRAYER OF THE FAITHFUL

(i) *Homily*

'The homily is a part of the liturgy, and is very strongly recommended. It is necessary nourishment for the Christian life. It should explain or throw light on some aspect of the readings from sacred scripture, or from another text of the Ordinary or Proper of the Mass, taking into consideration the mystery which is being celebrated and the particular needs of the listeners.

'At all Masses celebrated with the people on Sundays or feast days, there must be a homily. A homily is also recommended on other days, particularly the ferias of Advent, Lent and Paschal-time, as well as other feasts and occasions on which people more frequently come to church.

'The homily should normally be given by the celebrant himself' (GI, 41 and 42).

It is clear from this statement of the General Instruction, that we shall have to give the homily more careful consideration than in the past. Normally, it is not for a homily to last more than about seven minutes, but a great deal can be done in that time. Preparation—thorough preparation—is an absolute must. Periodic revision of one's manner and technique are also something we owe to those who listen, and this can best be done if we submit ourselves to the honest criticism of friends from differing backgrounds and walks of life. How easy it is for homilies to fall into a rut and remain there for years! With the spread and development of general education, and with the all-pervasive presence of television and radio, one wonders whether congregations will put up with this willingly as in the past. But what a wonderful opportunity the homily offers! Think of the preparation that goes into TV commercials and the money that advertisers are willing to pay for a thirty-second advertisement. You might feel that this is a poor comparison, but the underlying point remains valid : the homily offers an opportunity to help people understand the mystery of Christ and his Church and to see what it means in terms of the lives they lead and the people with whom they work, talk and relax. It assists them in bringing Christ to the world. If it offers an opportunity, it also brings responsibility. This responsibility responds to the Christian's right by baptism to be nourished by the word of God, and the duty of all Christians to seek the meaning of this word for themselves today, a duty which is particularly binding on those appointed by Christ as teachers in his Church.

The homily should not become a theology lecture. Its function is to illustrate the content of the scriptures and apply them to life as experienced by this or that particular congregation. It is one of the most important ways of bringing men to understand that God's plan of salvation is being worked out here and now, and, by eucharistic communion in Christ's sacrifice, to live out the mystery of Christ in their lives.

(ii) *Creed*

'The creed, or profession of faith, has this function in the celebration of Mass : that having heard the word of God in the readings and through the homily, the assembled people should respond and express their assent, and that they should recall the Church's faith to their minds before they celebrate the Eucharist' (GI, 43).

Historically, the creed or symbol of faith, has always been a text of the people. It is the baptismal profession which prepares us for the sacrifice of the Mass. Integrity of faith was always a necessary requisite for participation in the strictly eucharistic celebration.

'The creed is to be said by the priest together with the people on Sundays and solemnities. It may also be said in celebrations of particular solemnity.

'If it is sung, it is usually to be sung either by all or alternately' (GI, 44).

(iii)   *Prayers of the faithful or Bidding Prayers*

'In the universal prayer, or prayer of the faithful, the people, exercising their priestly role, pray for all men. It is fitting that this prayer should normally be included in Masses celebrated with the people, so that intercession may be made for the Church, for those holding public authority, for those in various kinds of need, for all men and for the salvation of the whole world' (GI, 45).

'Faithful' in this context refers, as its historical origins show, to the baptized as opposed to the unbaptized, not to the laity as opposed to the clergy. This prayer is a prayer of the whole of God's people assembled together in this worshipping community. In making this prayer in and through Christ, the whole assembly exercise that share in Christ's priesthood which is common to all the baptized.

The General Instruction emphasizes the importance of the prayers of the faithful even more than previous documents had done. These prayers are to be considered not as an optional extra, but as a normal part of the Mass. They have an important part to play in making the worshipping community aware both of the general needs of man and the Church and the concrete needs of those among whom the worshippers live and work. We see this from the list of intentions given in the Instruction :

'The series of intentions will normally be :
a)   for the needs of the Church;
b)   for civil authorities and for the well-being of the whole world;
c)   for those undergoing hardships, of whatever nature;
d)   for the local community.
'In special celebrations such as Confirmation, Marriages and Funerals, the order of the intentions may be altered to focus more closely on the particular occasion' (GI, 46).

This is not intended as a rigid unalterable list, but as a guideline. The underlying principle is that the prayers should not become 'parochial' in the negative sense, but should open out to the dimensions of the entire world. At the same time, explicit mention of sick people in the area, or of marriages, elections or local events that are important to the people present, brings the prayer alive in a way nothing else can. The requests for prayers for the sick of the parish, formerly made in the announcements etc., would now normally be included in the prayer of the faithful.

If the prayers of the faithful are to fulfil their function they must be carefully prepared. This demands imagination and effort. This effort will be compensated by the results, but if the prayers are always the same at this point of the Mass, they can become very burdensome. In some circumstances members of the local community—family groups for example—may be able to help the priest in preparing these prayers. Where this help is available and willingly offered, surely there are few priests who would object?

Another consideration is the way the prayers are actually conducted :

'It is for the celebrating priest to preside over the prayer. By a brief introduction he invites the faithful to pray, and afterwards he concludes with a prayer. It is fitting that the actual intentions should be said or sung by a deacon, cantor, or some other member of the faithful. The whole assembly expresses its prayer either by a common invocation after each intention, or by silent prayer' (GI, 47).

This way of conducting the prayer reflects the nature of the prayer as an intercession by the people of God, hierarchically organized with different functions and ministries.

7. ACTUAL CELEBRATION OF THE LITURGY OF THE WORD

The Readings

The readings before the Gospel, two on a Sunday and one on a weekday as a general rule, are given from the lectern. The lectern, reading-desk or ambo, as it is sometimes called, should normally be a stable fitting and 'placed so as to facilitate easy sight and sound on the part of the assembly' (GI, 272). Since the lectern is the place where the liturgy of the word is conducted, every care should be taken that it may express the respect we have for the word of God. From a practical point of view it should not be so high as to obscure the face of a man of medium height, and the lighting should be so arranged as neither to dazzle people looking towards the lectern, nor to leave shadows across the pages of the lectionary. The General Instruction points out that, as a general rule, commentators and leaders of song should not stand at the lectern but in some other place where they can exercise their office effectively. In this way the lectern will be regarded as the point at which God's word is proclaimed, just as the altar is specifically for the eucharistic liturgy. There are, however, many parish churches where the lectern would be the only practical place.

The readings will normally be read by lay-readers or lectors, or by a sub-deacon when there is one. The celebrant meanwhile is seated and listening to the reading with the rest of the assembly. The use of lay-readers is widespread by now, and where care is taken in helping the reader to master the basic communication techniques the effect is very good. Some dioceses have launched training schemes for lectors, with a considerable degree of success. Likewise, the training of priests and deacons in public speaking (cf chapter VI below) is now being given more care than in the past.

The reader announces the end of the reading with the words 'This is the word of the Lord' and the people reply 'Thanks be to God'. Apart from making it clear where the reading ends, this will also avoid the incongruity which sometimes arises when 'Thanks be to God' immediately follows the reading.

Where circumstances permit—but I cannot think of many parish situations which do—a silent pause is allowed after the reading, for quiet meditation. This is much more easily done in small group Masses or religious communities.

The Songs between the Readings

'The psalms which follow the first reading make most sense when they are sung. They should be proclaimed in such a way that their words can be heard and reflected upon. Unlike the other uses of psalmody in the Mass, where the psalm accompanies a procession (e.g. entrance, communion), this psalm is sung for its own sake.'[19]

[19] Music Advisory Board to the U.S. Bishops, *op. cit.*

'The cantor of the psalm, or the psalmist, at the lectern or in some other suitable place sings or says the verses of the psalm, with the whole congregation sitting and listening. The congregation normally takes part by saying or singing the responses or refrains, unless the psalm is sung or said straight through without a response.

'If this part of the Mass is in fact sung, then instead of the psalm given in the lectionary, there may be used either a gradual from the Roman Gradual or a responsorial psalm from the Simple Gradual, as described in those same books' (GI, 36).

Even when read it would seem preferable to have the psalm read by an individual or by the lector, with the people coming in with the refrain or response.

If the responsorial psalm is not sung, it must be said. The Alleluia and versicle before the Gospel may be omitted if they are not sung. The sequences, except on the days of Easter and Pentecost, are optional (GI, 39 and 40).

The Gospel

The high point of the liturgy of the word; all should stand while the Gospel is read.

'The highest veneration should be given to the reading of the Gospel. The liturgy itself teaches us this, showing that it is held in even higher honour than the other readings. It shows this in the blessing or prayer with which the deputed minister prepares himself, in the action of the faithful, who acknowledge and proclaim through their acclamations that Christ is present and speaking to them, and stand to listen to the reading, and in the signs of respect given to the book of Gospels itself' (GI, 35).

The Gospel is read at the lectern by a deacon, if there is one, or by a priest if there is not. When there is a deacon he asks the priest's blessing, saying in a subdued voice 'Father, give me your blessing' and the priest in a subdued voice says, 'The Lord be in your heart and on your lips that you may worthily proclaim his Gospel; in the name of the Father and of the Son and of the Holy Spirit.' The deacon replies, 'Amen.' If there is no deacon, the priest himself bows before the altar and says silently,

'Almighty God, cleanse my heart and my lips that I may worthily proclaim your Gospel.' Then the deacon or priest goes to the lectern (or pulpit). He may be accompanied by ministers with incense and candles (he takes the book of Gospels from the altar if it has been there at the beginning of Mass, but if there is only a full lectionary in use the lectionary will already be on the lectern). The deacon or priest then says 'The Lord be with you' and the people answer, 'And also with you.' He goes on : 'A reading from the Holy Gospel according to (Luke)' and meanwhile he makes the sign of the cross on the book of the Gospels and then on himself, on his forehead, lips and breast. The people reply, 'Glory to you, O Lord.' If incense is to be used the deacon or priest incenses the book of the Gospels (or lectionary) and then he proclaims the Gospel. At the end of the Gospel the deacon or priest says 'This is the Gospel of the Lord' and the people reply, 'Praise be to you O Christ.' The deacon or priest then kisses the book of the Gospels, saying silently, 'By the word of the Gospel may our sins be blotted out.'

Homily

This is given either at the seat or the lectern (GI, 97). It may be followed by a period of silence during which each member of the assembly reflects on the word of God and the celebrant's homily upon it.

Profession of faith

The celebrant will normally be at the seat when this is said, since it is normally at the seat that the prayer of the faithful follows. The General Instruction indicates a profound bow at the words 'And was made man' (GI, 98 and 234). On the feast of the Annunciation and at Christmas there is a genuflection instead of a profound bow (GI, 98).

Prayers of the faithful

We have already described the way the prayer is celebrated (p. 77 above). The celebrant will normally be at the seat, with a minister or lay-reader at the lectern.

CHAPTER V

The Eucharistic Liturgy

'The Last Supper, in which Christ instituted the memorial of his death and resurrection, is continually made present in the Church when the priest, representing Christ Our Lord, accomplishes what Christ did and commanded his disciples to do in memory of him, thereby instituting the sacrifice and paschal meal.

'Christ in fact took the bread and the cup, gave thanks, broke the bread and gave the bread and the cup to his disciples, saying: Take, eat, drink; this is my Body; this is my Blood. Do this in memory of me. Accordingly the Church so arranged the eucharistic liturgy that its various parts correspond to the words and actions of Christ. Therefore:

i.   in the preparation of the gifts, the bread, wine and water are all brought to the altar. These are the same elements that Christ took into his hands;

ii.   in the eucharistic prayer, thanks is given to God for the whole work of salvation, and the offerings become the Body and Blood of Christ;

iii.   The unity of the faithful is shown by the breaking of the one bread; in communion the faithful receive the Body and Blood of the Lord just as the apostles did from the hands of Christ himself' (GI, 48).

We have here a clear presentation of the eucharistic liturgy in relation to the actions and words of Our Lord at the Last

Supper. Many will find this passage helpful as a point of departure for catechesis on this subject. It shows how the three sections
of the eucharistic liturgy are inseparably linked and only understood in relation to each other. We shall treat each of these
three sections in turn. In each case we shall offer points regarding
the significance of the section in question and a description of its
actual celebration. Although for the sake of clarity we make a
distinction between significance and celebration, at many points
in our commentary these two aspects overlap.

1. PREPARATION OF THE GIFTS

i. *Background*

This part of the Mass had not been touched in the preceding
reform, but now it has been revised so as to make its meaning
clearer and more straightforward. The title 'Preparation of the
gifts' indicates what is essential to this part of the Mass, namely
the bringing forward of the gifts of bread and wine and placing
them on the altar in preparation for their consecration in the
eucharistic prayer. The term 'offertory' is an accurate description
if it is understood as applying to the actual bringing forward of
the gifts which are to be consecrated. It is inaccurate if it is taken
to imply that this is an offering of the gifts over and above their
sacrificial offering in the eucharistic prayer, and this explains the
changes which have now been made : those prayers have been
removed or changed which seemed to anticipate the eucharistic
prayer itself and which tended to obscure the essential meaning
of this part of the rite.

The offertory of the Mass—the preparation of the gifts—has
a long and complex history in the Roman rite.[1] In the first two
centuries, the bringing forward of the materials for the sacrificial
meal was accompanied by little or no ceremonial. As the custom
grew of the faithful bringing their own bread and wine for the
sacrifice an offertory procession developed, and this continued
for more than a thousand years in the Western liturgies. Nor did

a) CHANGE OF NAME

b) HISTORY

(i)

(ii)

---

[1] For a detailed account of the history of the offertory rite, cf Joseph
Jungmann, *The Mass of the Roman Rite,* Burnes & Oates, London 1959,
pp. 315–62; N. M. Denis-Boulet, 'La Liturgie Eucharistique : L'Offertoire',
in *L'Eglise en Prière,* ed. A. Mortimort, Descleé and Cie, Tournai 1961,
pp. 362–79.

they bring bread and wine alone. Other gifts of food and utilities were added to the bread and wine—gifts for the support of the clergy or the poor and for the maintenance of the Church. By the twelfth century these other gifts had largely given way to a straight contribution in money.

The offertory procession had also become more and more rare. (iii) The spread of a more monastic liturgy, the drop in the frequency of communion, and the introduction of unleavened bread in the early middle ages were probably among the many factors responsible for this. The chant that had accompanied the procession was also drastically shortened, and all that was left was the present-day offertory antiphon. The music accompanying the text of this antiphon became, as time went on, more and more beyond the capabilities of the normal congregation, and motets sung by highly-trained choirs were gradually introduced. Even before the disappearance of the offertory procession, prayers began to be inserted to accompany the actions of the priest at the altar. These prayers varied from church to church.[2] The Missal of Pius V in 1570, the Missal which we have been using up to the present day, made a selection from among these many variants.

(iv) The Liturgy Consilium embarked on the reform of the offertory in an attempt to clarify the meaning of this part of the rite. First of all, it had to eliminate elements which anticipated and duplicated the eucharistic prayer. It did this in accordance with the principles of *The Constitution on the Liturgy* that parts of the Mass, 'which with the passage of time came to be duplicated, or were added with little advantage, are to be omitted' (art. 50). The first draft of the reform reduced the offertory rite to its three principal elements: the bringing of the gifts to the altar (preferably by a procession), the placing of the gifts on the altar, and the prayer over these gifts. Later modifications of these first drafts have retained many of the other elements, but these three remain primary in importance.

ii. *Significance*

a) *Procession, placing of gifts on the altar, prayer over the* (i) *gifts:* The procession by which members of the congregation bring

[2] Johannes Bauer, *Liturgical Handbook for Holy Mass,* Newman Press, Maryland 1961, p. 73.

up the gifts of bread and wine from the nave to the altar is
strongly emphasized in the new Order of the Mass (GI, 49). It
is important because it signifies the active participation of the
whole assembly in the sacrificial action, the sacred meal, which is
to take place. It is both an exercise and an expression of the
priesthood of the faithful. Speaking of the offertory procession
as it was in the past, Fr Clifford Howell has said :

> 'The right to provide bread and wine was strictly reserved
> for those in full membership of the Church. Only those who
> had a right to communicate had also the right to offer;
> exclusion from the communion meant exclusion from offering.
> Providing bread and wine, therefore, was allied to the general
> priesthood of the faithful, even though only the ordained could
> consecrate, all baptized (whether ordained or not) could offer,
> and all who offered should provide. Hence the provision of the
> sacrificial elements was both a manifestation and an exercise
> of the general priesthood.'[3]

The placing of the gifts on the altar to be consecrated and then
consumed by those who brought them up, is already a sign that
they are set apart for sacrifice. It is impossible to think of this
preparation of the gifts except as leading up to the point where
they are to be consecrated and consumed. As Hippolytus said
of this rite in the third century :

> 'Then the oblation will be presented by the deacons to the
> bishop and he will give thanks, over the bread that it might be
> the symbol of the Body of Christ, over the cup of mixed wine
> that it might be the image of the Blood which was poured out
> for all those who believe in him.'[4]

As so often in the liturgy the action is accompanied by a prayer
which clarifies its meaning : the prayer over the gifts.

> 'The bread and wine placed upon the altar to be consecrated
> were dedicated by a special "prayer over the gifts"; it was the

---

[3] Clifford Howell, 'Reforming the Liturgy : The Offertory', *Clergy Review,*
June 1967, p. 468.

[4] To avoid misunderstanding, it should perhaps be pointed out that the
use of 'image' and 'symbol' here must be understood in their context. They
are in no sense a denial of the truth of Christ's presence, but a way of
describing his sacramental presence, which frequently occurs in patristic
literature.

prerogative of the celebrant, as representing the Church, to accept these gifts and assign them for sacrificial use. His act and his prayer were thus a manifestation and an exercise of the mediatorship of the Church.'[5]

b) Reflecting on the *significance of the presentation of the gifts,* Fr Robert Ledogar has suggested that

'it is fundamentally a thanksgiving for the gifts of creation or, better perhaps, an acknowledgement of the material universe as gift to man. This means, of course, that the bread and wine are seen as symbolic realities prior to their transformation in the eucharistic blessing. What do they symbolize? They can symbolize a number of things according to the cultural context; but, precisely as the elements of a thanksgiving meal of discipleship, they signify that whatever man uses as sign and source of communion with God and his brothers is already God's gift to him. They signify, in other words, that everything is gift. Life is a gift, self is a gift, existence is a gift. We do not take all this for granted and look for salvation to come from somewhere outside the created order. We see and acknowledge "the goodness and kindness of God our saviour" already in the universe at the root of matter itself, waiting to "come into the world" not as though from outside, but as gradually manifested, as an epiphany.'[6]

There are a number of ideas here: firstly, that the original meal-context of the eucharist underlines the fact that 'any food taken with grateful acknowledgement of its source is an offering to God';[7] secondly, that the bread and wine are taken as signs of God's presence in the universe and of his ordering of it for man;[8] thirdly, that, as the new prayers accompanying the placing of the bread and wine on the altar emphasize, these 'fruits of creation' have also become the work of men's hands. In bringing these gifts forward, man's co-operation with God's work of creation is clearly underlined, and man acknowledges that all he has and is comes from God. Fourthly, bringing these gifts is acknowledgement of God's Lordship over him and over all

---

[5] Clifford Howell, *art. cit.,* p. 468.
[6] Robert J. Ledogar, 'The Eucharistic Prayer and the Gifts over Which it is Spoken', *Worship* 41 (December 1967) p. 592.
[7] *Ibid.,* p. 589.
[8] *Ibid.,* p. 594.

creation and in response to God's love, man 'rightly offers back
the first fruits of creation, not as though God needed them, but
as signs of his own gratitude'.[9] This attitude is the heart of all
true worship, of all true sacrifice, and therefore illustrates the
spirit that should accompany preparation for the sacrifice. Fifthly,
in bringing these gifts to the altar, in order that the eucharist
might be celebrated over them, the bread and wine are taken
into another dimension. Not only is creation revealed as being
for man, and not only is man's relationship to his creator acknowledged, but the ordering of all things to Christ as their centre
and purpose is openly declared. He, the Word through whom all
things were made, is the Word made flesh in whom all creation
finds its meaning. When Christians bring forward the bread and
wine they bring them forward as the materials of the one, true,
life-giving sacrifice of Christ. These gifts which are the sign of
God's presence in the universe, and of his ordering of it towards
man becomes, through the eucharistic prayer, signs of God's self-
emptying, redeeming love of man.[10] Christians bring these gifts
forward in order that through Christ's own sacrifice they might
become the signs of God's own love for man and of man's
response to God in and with Christ. Sixthly, we can see how the
presence of Christ is gradually revealed in the celebration of the
eucharist, and how through the eucharistic prayer this presence
is most fully realized in the presence of the risen Christ among
his own in a spirit of fellowship.

c) *Practical conclusions regarding the bread:* What has been
said regarding the significance of the rite has practical consequences. It is not a question here of theorizing which has nothing
to do with the practical realities of parish Masses. The liturgy is
the language of the sign, and it is of maximum importance that
the signs should actually signify, that they should be expressive
and effective. The sacramental signs affect the faith of men, and
the efficacy of the sacrament is intextricably bound up with the
quality of the sign. So the more that the sacramental signs are
seen as such, the more deeply they are understood, the more fully
a person responds, the more thorough-going the effect of the
sacrament is likely to be.

[9] *Ibid.,* p. 590.
[10] *Ibid.,* p. 594.

It follows that the procession with the gifts, the placing of them on the altar, and the prayer over them should stand out clearly. It also explains why almost every document dealing with the reform of the Mass from the time of Pius XII's *Mediator Dei* in 1947 has urged that the hosts that are to be used for communion be those presented and consecrated at the same Mass. If this is done, communion is more clearly understood as the sharing in *this* celebration, *this* Mass, and is seen as sharing in the gifts that have been presented and offered in sacrifice to the Father and accepted by him. It is certainly difficult to calculate the exact numbers of communicants, but communion from hosts consecrated at that Mass can be achieved for the greater number of Sunday Masses, and it is possible to distribute at any Mass at least some hosts which were presented and consecrated at that Mass.

Another practical conclusion is found in the General Instruction on celebration of Mass where it states that

'the sign aspect requires that the materials for the eucharistic celebration should be seen to be real food. It is necessary therefore that the eucharistic bread, even though it is unleavened, should be made in such a way that when celebrating Mass with a congregation the priest is able to break it into different pieces and distribute it to at least some of the people. Small hosts are in no way excluded when the numbers receiving communion, and other pastoral reasons, make such a solution necessary. But the breaking of the bread—as the eucharist was known in apostolic times—openly demonstrates the power and importance of the sign of the unity of all in the one bread, and of love when this bread is distributed among the brothers' (GI, 283).

There are a growing number of places where a thicker type of bread has begun to be used, and this can be so made as to break easily into pieces for communion.[11] Not many parish priests, however, have the time to go looking round for this type of altar-bread, and liturgy commissions give a very useful service when they give information of where such bread is to be obtained, how it can be broken quickly and efficiently, and in general how

[11] See p. 127, regarding the 'fraction' or breaking of bread.

practical difficulties in this field can best be kept to a minimum while giving full scope to the aspect of sign mentioned above.

d) *The collection:* Money is something that looms large in the lives of all those gathered to celebrate the Mass, and not least of all in the life of the parish priest/pastor. There are black moments when it looms so large as to block the vision of all else! It is not out of place then that the function of money in the life of the Christian community should find some expression in the Mass. In these days of planned giving, there is less need for numerous collections at Mass, but in most places a collection during the offertory remains. Often enough the collection is for a specific purpose or need. But the collection must be integrated into the Mass, it should not be regarded as a regrettable intrusion which has nothing to do with our being at Mass. Obviously, this does not just depend on the way the collection is carried out in the Mass, it depends on the way money is acquired, used and distributed in each diocese, and what happens at Mass will depend on this being done equably and efficiently. We give a few points here as to how the collection can relate to the Mass.[12]

The collection, as GI, 49 points out, is best related to the offertory procession. It is suggested that while the altar is being prepared, the collection is taken. Whether this is a practical possibility will obviously depend on local circumstances. If ways could be found of doing this rapidly both this collection and any planned giving envelopes gathered before Mass begins could be taken up in the procession of gifts. The collection should be presented as being equivalent to the individual's own sacrificial self-offering, since this is something more than the money he offers—it is effected in the union with Christ's sacrifice, and thanks to his sacrifice, which comes with the presentation, consecration and consumption of the gifts of bread and wine. There is no reason however why the money-offering should not be taken as part-expression of the desire to offer oneself and all one has to God, and is indeed a very concrete expression of a man's desire to 'put his body where his mouth is'. If a man is serious about this, his

[12] For a fuller treatment of this subject, see Joseph C. Buckley, 'Money and the Offertory', and Duncan Cloud, 'The Theology of the Offertory Collection', both in *The Mass and the People of God*, ed. James Crichton, Burns & Oates, London 1966.

offering to the collection will be in proportion to his possibilities and responsibilities, and to the need in question. The spirit in which this is done is all-important. By this money-offering, it is not as if Christians paid God his due and thus 'earned' God's gratitude and praise! The parable of the pharisee and the publican illustrates a recurring temptation. When the Christian comes to give worship to God, any money-offering which expresses his desire to offer himself in union with Christ is an expression of gratitude to God, acknowledging that we have come from him, and all is his. It is another partial explicitation of what we said above regarding the symbolism of the bread and wine. We are stewards of all God has given us, and unprofitable stewards at that. Our hope is in Christ in whom all things have their meaning, and all things have their fulfilment. Duncan Cloud has underlined an important aspect of the collection, in stressing it as a symbol of common fellowship in Christ. Here too, it links up with the fellowship of the sacrificial meal. If petitions in the prayer of the faithful are directly linked with *this* collection, if the fellowship of those entering through communion more deeply into the sacrifice of Christ is linked with common social action outside of Mass along the same avenue indicated by the bidding prayers and collection—it may well be that the assembly will become more aware of itself as a community in Christ.

The Mass is not something floating around outside space and time, it must always be related to the lives of those taking part, even if through the presence of Christ it reaches out across history. Awareness of fellowship in Christ must always take men beyond the bounds of the present assembly gathered to celebrate the Mass, and involve them in concern, care, and respect for others. The collection can be a concrete expression of this. But again, remembering the publican and the pharisee, let it not be made in a patronizing or paternalistic way, but as a sharing in gratitude of the gifts that God has given, building rather than destroying men's self-respect, gratefully sharing above all the love which the Father gives us in the Body and Blood of his Son.

iii.   *Actual celebration of the rite*

    a)   *Singing and silence:* Whether one of these two elements is to predominate at this point will depend on the nature of

the particular celebration. In general it will often be better to
give the congregation a period of quiet here.

'Let the congregation just watch in a prayerful spirit. They ①
have already done much singing or answering; they have
listened to the scripture reading and homily, have professed
their faith, and have taken part in the bidding prayers. Now
they need some relaxation of attention, a kind of pause before
the real spiritual and psychological effort of attending closely
to the great eucharistic prayer and "offering themselves as
spiritual victims with and through the High Priest himself"
(*Mediator Dei*, no. 105).'[13]

Singing then is not always necessary or desirable at this point.
Organ or instrumental music can be very useful in helping people
to relax and in creating a prayerful contemplative mood.

When it is judged desirable to sing, it should be remembered
that 'the proper function of this song is to accompany and cele- ②
brate the communal aspects of the procession'.[14] The offertory
antiphon may be used with a psalm in the same way as described
above for the entrance antiphon. When the offertory antiphon
is not sung, it is omitted (GI, 50). If other texts are used, they
can be any appropriate song of praise or rejoicing in keeping with
the liturgical season. They do not have to refer explicitly to the
bread and wine, and indeed if they do they should make the
reference in a way suitable to *this* point of the Mass rather than
to the eucharistic prayer, communion, or even eucharistic benediction. If there is singing during the procession and the placing
of the gifts on the altar, it could often be left to the choir. 'In
any case, all music should, of course, cease in time for the prayer
over the gifts which is the original and only essential priestly
prayer, and a fitting conclusion to the preparatory rite leading to
the eucharistic sacrifice itself.'[15]

b) *Preparation of the altar; the collection:* Once the prayers
of the faithful are over, ministers or altar-servers bring the
corporal, purificator, chalice and missal (or sacramentary) and
place them on the altar.

[13] Clifford Howell, 'Reforming the Liturgy: The Offertory', *Clergy
Review*, June 1967, p. 471.
[14] Statement of Music Advisory Board to the U.S. Bishops, *op. cit.*
[15] Clifford Howell, *art. cit.*, p. 471.

The collection could be taken at this point. If ways could be found of doing this rapidly, the collected money could be taken up in procession together with the gifts. This would both express its meaning more clearly, avoid making the preparation of gifts appear as merely a pause for the collection, and allow people a period of quiet prayer. The fact remains, however, that in perhaps the majority of parishes it will be physically impossible to do this in the time unless the priest waits for the collection to be brought up before going on. The degree to which this is possible without prolonging the Mass unduly, will depend on the number of people, size of the church, etc.

c) *Procession with gifts:*

'It is desirable that the participation of the faithful should be manifested through the presentation of the bread and wine for the eucharistic celebration, or of other gifts to be used for the needs of the Church and the poor.

'The offerings of the faithful may be accepted by the priest, helped by the ministers, and put in a suitable place. The bread and the wine for the celebration are taken to the altar' (GI, 101).

It helps to concentrate attention on the procession itself if the priest is seen to be concentrating on it and waiting to receive the gifts. It will also involve the congregation more, if the people who bring up the gifts are varied rather than always being the same group of people. Whole families can bring up the gifts.

d) *The placing of the bread on the altar:* The priest takes the paten with the bread, and holding it above the altar says the new prayer which accompanies it. This prayer is a combination of a prayer taken from the Jewish meal ritual and the concept of man's work consecrated to the Lord, an idea which the Pope himself wanted to be expressed in some way at this point of the Mass:

'Blessed are you, Lord, God of all creation.
Through your goodness we have this bread to offer,
which earth has given and human hands have made.
It will become for us the bread of life.'

He then replaces the paten on the corporal.

When there is no singing the priest can say the prayer out loud, and the congregation can reply : 'Blessed be God for ever' (OMP, 19). The prayer may also be said silently.

e) *The mixing of the water and wine:* The priest, standing at the side of the altar, takes the wine from the server and pours some into the chalice; he then adds some water, without making any sign of the cross over the water. If the mixing of the wine and water is done by a deacon, it may be done either at the side of the altar or at the credence table before handing the chalice to the priest. The prayer accompanying this action is said silently. This prayer retains the essential elements of the former prayer at this point, and is based on an ancient Roman Christmas oration which refers to the union of the human and divine natures in Christ and our own union with him :

'By the mystery of this water and wine, may we come to share in his divinity, who humbled himself to share in our humanity.'

The symbolism of water, and the symbolism worked into the mixing of the wine and water, aroused many fierce controversies in the first millenium of Christianity. A generally accepted symbolism is illustrated by Fr Jungmann :

'The mixing of the water with the wine symbolizes the intimate union of the faithful with him to whom they have bound themselves in faith; and this union is so firm that nothing can separate it, just as the water can no longer be separated from the wine. From this, Cyprian concludes: "When someone offers only wine, then the blood of Christ begins to exist without us; but when it is only water, then the people begin to exist without Christ".'[16]

This particular symbolism may seem far-fetched today, but the theological principles it expresses remain perfectly valid.

f) *The placing of the chalice on the altar:* The priest takes the chalice in which there is now wine and water and says a prayer of 'Blessing' similar to that said over the bread :

[16] Joseph Jungmann, *op. cit.,* p. 333, where he quotes Cyprian, Ep. 63, *Ad Caecilium.*

'Blessed are you, Lord, God of all creation.
Through your goodness we have this wine to offer,
fruit of the vine and work of human hands.
It will become our spiritual drink.'

Both this formula, and that over the bread, contain the following concepts: gift of God, work of man, fruit of the earth, and the desire for their acceptance and consecration by God. Like the prayer over the bread, this may be said out loud if there is no singing, and an acclamation by the congregation is also allowed (OMP, 21). The priest then replaces the chalice on the corporal. There is a departure here from the rubrics of the past: it is no longer stated that the chalice must be placed behind the paten. They can be side by side. The other receptacles for communion hosts and wine may also be placed in whatever way is most convenient. Regarding the paten, the General Instruction states that it is perfectly in order to use one wide paten in which the bread for the celebrants, as well as for the ministers and faithful, can be contained (GI, 293). This will be particularly useful if the bread is so made as to be broken for distribution in small particles at the communion; a small rim round the edge would prevent pieces from falling off when distributing communion, and a short stem would make it easier to hold.

The use of a pall for covering the chalice or chalices is now optional (GI, 103).

The beautiful prayer 'In spiritu humilitatis' has been retained since it so aptly expresses what our dispositions should be as we approach the sacrifice. The priest bows and says the prayer silently.

g) *Incensation:* At this point there can be incensations if these are judged suitable for this particular celebration.

'The gifts on the altar, and the altar itself, may be incensed in order to signify that the offering of the Church and its prayer rise like incense before God. When the gifts and altar have been incensed, the priest and people may be incensed by the deacon or minister (server)' (GI, 51).

The way the incensations are carried out is described on p. 40.

h) *Washing of hands:* The priest then washes his hands—whether incense has been used or not—at the side of the altar.

This rite expresses the desire for internal purification (GI, 52) and the priest says silently verse 4 of psalm 50 :

'Lord, wash away my sin; cleanse me from my iniquity.'

i) *Orate Fratres and prayer over the gifts:*

'Having returned to the middle of the altar, standing facing the people, extending and joining his hands, the priest invites the people to prayer, saying: "Pray, brethren, . . ." After the people's response, with his hands extended he says the prayer over the gifts. At the end of this the people say : Amen' (GI, 107).

This is an example of where the prayer and response can be 'made' or 'ruined' by the celebrant. In addressing the people, it is natural that he should calmly, and without either stiffness or slovenliness, extend his hands, gradually drawing them together as the people respond. It is courtesy to the congregation to wait for their response before looking in the altar book for the prayer over the gifts. His gestures, his eyes, his attention must all be focused on the meaning of what he is doing.

The prayer over the gifts is that of the Mass of the day, if it is proper. On the memorial days of the saints it can be taken from the Mass of the common or from the ferial Mass, unless the prayer is proper to the saint. On ferial days 'per annum' there is a choice betwen the prayers over the gifts of the thirty-four Sundays or those of the Masses and Prayers for various occasions (GI, 323).

The prayer over the gifts has now only a short conclusion, 'through Christ Our Lord' (GI, 32).

A short pause before the 'Lord be with you' of the eucharistic prayer is an extremely useful psychological break, and allows attention to be refocused when the central prayer of the Mass begins.

2. THE EUCHARISTIC PRAYER

'Now the eucharistic prayer, the centre and summit of the entire celebration, actually begins. It is a prayer of thanksgiving and consecration. The priest invites the people to lift their hearts to God in prayer and thanksgiving and associates them with him in the prayer, which, in the name of the whole community, he addresses to God the Father through Jesus Christ. The meaning and purpose of this prayer is that the entire congregation of the faithful should unite themselves with Christ in acknowledging all the wonderful things God has done and in offering the sacrifice' (GI, 54).

It is obvious from this statement that any presentation of the Mass to people must pay careful attention to the understanding of the eucharistic prayer. For that reason, we shall dwell on it for the moment under four headings : i) background and origins, ii) structure and content; iii) the four eucharistic prayers we have today; iv) actual celebration.

i)   *Background and origins*
When speaking of the presentation of gifts we spoke of the formulas accompanying the placing of bread and wine on the altar as 'Blessings' in the tradition of Jewish-Christian prayer. When we speak of the eucharistic prayer we shall come back to that term 'Blessing' because the four New Testament accounts of the institution of the eucharist are unanimous in stating that Jesus pronounced a 'Blessing' over the bread and wine which he made the sacramental signs of the sacrifice. They use the Greek verbs *eucharistein* and *eulogein* which mean 'to thank' and 'to praise', thus interpreting the meaning of the Hebrew word *berakah* or 'blessing'. The Hebrews did not have a word for thanksgiving, but the evangelists were perfectly justified in interpreting it in this way because the word 'blessing' places us immediately in an atmosphere of praise and thanksgiving. This Jewish 'blessing' is essentially a prayer of response, response to the word of God. For the Jew this word was not something abstract but a living reality. The word of God implied the intervention of God in human history, the events by which Israel had been delivered from Egypt and formed into God's own people in the covenant of Sinai. In the mouth of the Jew the prayer of blessing was a public acknowledgement of what God had done for him, both as an individual and as a member of his people. It was a proclamation of his faith in God who loved him, and an expression of hope in the definitive salvation that God had promised. It was a prayer,

a response, of wonder and praise, joy and thanksgiving, to his God and saviour, his Father and creator.

The Old Testament is studded with examples of this type of prayer. For example we find the astonished cry of the servant led by the cousin of his master Abraham into the house of Nabor: 'Blessed be Yahweh, God of my master Abraham, for he has not stopped showing kindness and goodness to my master. Yahweh has guided my steps to the house of my master's brother' (Gen 24:27). We have the meeting of Jethro with his kinsman Moses (Ex 18:10–11), and the gratitude of David in his cry: 'Blessed be the Lord the God of Israel, who has granted that my eyes should today see one of my descendants seated on my throne' (1 Kg 1:48). This form of prayer finds its privileged expression in the book of Psalms, and blessing was quite naturally inserted into the liturgy of sacrifice. Moreover, in the blessing of a synagogue worship we find: the acclamation Sanctus, the recalling of the fathers, thanksgiving for the revelation of the name of God and the law, the memorial of the actions of God, the prayer for redemption, justice and peace, and the final doxology —all of these can be traced in the great eucharistic prayer.

In the New Testament we also find examples of the prayer of blessing. Perhaps the most well known is Our Lord's

'I bless you, Father, Lord of heaven and earth, for hiding these things from the learned and the clever and revealing them to mere children. Yes, Father, for that is what it pleased you to do. Everything has been entrusted to me by my Father; and no one knows the Son except the Father, just as no one knows the Father except the Son and those to whom the Son chooses to reveal him' (Mt 11:25–27).

It can be seen here how the actual praise and thanksgiving is followed by a statement of the motive for the thanksgiving. The same is true of the 'blessings' in the Pauline epistles, cf Eph 1:3–14. There are many types of this prayer of blessing, but a recurring pattern is the exclamation of praise and thanksgiving, followed by a statement of the motive for this, which in turn lead in to a prayer that God might renew or continue his actions in favour of his people or the individual. For the Jew this petition was not considered as something self-centred, since it was an acknowledgement of his total dependence on God and, as a prayer, that he might be able to receive what God himself wanted to give, the highest point of praise and thanksgiving. It was natural then that this should flow over into a concluding exclamation or hymn of praise : the doxology. The pattern which emerges is thus : *praise and thanksgiving, memorial, petition, doxology of praise*.

Of particular importance to us here is the Jews' use of blessings at meals, because it was in the course of a meal, 'while they were at the table eating' (Mk 14 : 17), that Jesus instituted the eucharist. The acknowledgement of God's goodness with gratitude is natural for someone who is about to receive his gifts, and the prayer of 'blessing', a 'eucharist' or thanksgiving, comes forward spontaneously. This is important if we are to understand the relationship between the eucharistic prayer and the gifts over which it is spoken :

> 'One who "blessed God" before taking bread was also considered to have "blessed the bread"; indeed "nothing is to be rejected if it is received with thanksgiving; for then it is consecrated by the word of God and prayer" (1 Tim 4 :4).'[17]

The Jewish meal ritual was particularly marked on festivals and sabbaths, but the paschal meal was the most important of them all and it is highly probable that the last supper was the celebration supper of the Passover, or Pasch.[18] It is at least certain that the meal took place during the period when the Passover was being celebrated, and it must be understood in the light of the event being celebrated.

But what was the Passover meal? It had its origins in two separate feasts : that of the shepherds which involved the sacrifice of a young lamb, and that of the agriculturalists who ate and sacrificed unleavened bread, first fruits of the harvest, which was not fermented with the previous year's grain. These two festivals were fused into the feast on which the Jews celebrated the time when God led them out of Egypt to establish with them the covenant of Sinai—that treaty of friendship by which they became his people and he was acknowledged as their saviour, their God. It was a celebration of the fact that they had been,

---

[17] Robert J. Ledogar, *art. cit.*, p. 587.
[18] Joachim Jeremias, *The Eucharistic Words of Jesus,* London and New York, 1966.

and continued to be, God's own people. The slaying of the lambs and the ritual meal were therefore situated in the temple, the sign of God's presence among his people. By the time of Our Lord sheer weight of numbers made it impossible for all to eat the paschal meal in the temple, and it was therefore celebrated in private homes or in the camps of pilgrims who had come up for the feast. The relationship between the slaying of the lamb in sacrifice and eating the paschal meal was not lost :

> 'At its heart, the eating of the paschal meal was that of a sacramental communion in the temple sacrifice of the paschal lamb. This was a communion-sacrifice in which those who ate were joyfully sharing in the act of worship performed in the sacrificial slaying of the lamb. Thus, the altar and table were not disparate or contradictory elements in the observance of the pasch, but were rather two moments of one sacramental act whose meaning bound them together. The eating of the paschal lamb was the sacramental communion in the sacramental meal of a sacrifice : the renewal in Israel of the religious event of the Exodus. In this act (sacrifice and eating of the sacrifice) the unity of the people was created by God as he shared the sacrifice with his people. Israel was once again released from the slavery of all that Egypt meant to them. Israel joyfully renewed her covenant with God and was made to be (once again, *in* this act) the people of God. Altar and table were bound into a sacramental unity by the central religious significance of the sacrifice of the paschal lamb.[19]

It is against this background that we must see Jesus' celebration of the paschal meal.

The ritual accompanying the paschal meal was colourful and elaborate, each detail reflecting an aspect of Israel's deliverance from Egypt. Here we focus our attention on three points : it was in the customary blessing at the beginning of the meal which accompanied the breaking and distribution of the bread that Jesus declared 'This is my Body, which is to be given for you' (Lk 22 :19). The sacrificial significance of these last words was heightened by the eating of the paschal lamb which followed— the paschal lamb slain on the altar of the temple which Jesus

[19] Joseph M. Power, *Eucharistic Theology,* Burnes & Oates/Herder and Herder, London 1968, p. 55.

③ was to replace on the altar of the cross. At the end of the meal there was the solemn celebration of what we would call 'grace after meals'. Jesus took the cup of wine into his hands and pronounced the three blessings which were traditional at this point in the ritual. The second and third of these blessings are especially important as a forerunner of the Christian eucharistic prayer. There we have prayers of gratitude and praise where we find not only a memorial of what God has done for his people in the events of the past, but also 'a supplication that the creative and redemptive action of God in olden times be continued and renewed today, and that it find its ultimate fulfilment in the coming of the Messiah and the final establishment of the kingdom of God'.[20] Jesus, presenting to his own the cup of wine, invites them to see there the fulfilment of this hope: 'This cup is the new covenant in my Blood' (1 Cor 11 : 25), 'which will be poured out for you' (Lk 22 : 20).

> 'Something of capital importance emerges from this paschal setting. It is the fact that the transformation which takes place is not simply the transformation of a piece of bread. It is rather transformation of the religious meaning and power of the *unleavened bread eaten in the paschal meal.* It is the transformation of the sacrificial meaning and power of the Unleavened Bread. Rather than invoking the reality of the sacrifice of the paschal lamb in the unity of the paschal table with the altar in the temple, eating of this bread now evokes the reality of a sacrifice which is timelessly present in the person of Jesus. Drinking from this cup now means and is participation in the new covenant which God has given to man in Jesus. It means the constantly renewed gift of belonging to that people whom God has created in Jesus.'[21]

ii.   Development of the eucharistic prayer

① Since in early Christian times the eucharist was celebrated at the end of a meal in common, it was only natural that the two blessings of the original Lord's supper, those at the beginning and end of the meal, should come to be united in one prayer of

---

[20] Louis Bouyer, *The Eucharist,* University of Notre Dame Press, Indiana, 1968, p. 83.
[21] Joseph M. Power, *op. cit.,* pp. 57–8.

blessing. This prayer of blessing, from which the later eucharistic prayers were developed, took much of its character from the blessings at the end of the paschal meal referred to above. The connection is particularly evident in the second and third of these blessings with their features of praise and thanksgiving, memorial and intercession.

Within the general structure of the eucharistic blessing, there was a great deal of room for improvisation and for composition, and in the first three centuries there were no fixed or official texts. We have a clear description of the celebration of the eucharist in this period in the Apology of Justin Martyr, and an outline of the content of the eucharistic prayer in the *Apostolic Tradition* of Hippolytus. From the fourth century onwards, however, there was a general tendency to use fixed formulas, and as time went on these became accepted as 'official'. This tendency began in the Eastern Churches, and the principal reason seems to have been to ensure orthodoxy in the face of heresies such as Arianism. There was considerable variety on the basic eucharistic theme, and within the Christian world, two main types of eucharistic prayer gradually emerged : those stemming from Alexandria and those stemming from Antioch. This further diversified into five main 'families' : the Egyptian or Alexandrine; the Antioch or West Syrian tradition; the East Syrian; the Roman; and the Gallican and Spanish.

In all these types of eucharistic prayer an essential nucleus is discernible : after the hymn of praise and thanksgiving for all that God has done for us, there is the account of the words and gestures of Our Lord at the Last Supper, the memorial of Christ's redemptive work, the prayer that the bread and wine may become the Body and Blood of Christ, and that in this way the narrative and memorial may be effective for the Church and for all those participating in the offerings. Other elements, such as the Sanctus, the commemoration of the saints and the various intercessions, were gradually added as time went on.

The arrangement of the various elements within the eucharistic prayer varied according to the different traditions. Moreover, the Oriental rites had a number of anaphoras, but the actual text of each anaphora was fixed and unvaried. In the Spanish and Gallican traditions, the text of the anaphora varied according to the feast, and the variant prefaces and Hanc Igiturs of the Roman

Canon show the same tendency to vary according to the different seasons of the liturgical cycle.

The use of the Roman Canon gradually extended, and by the eleventh century it was the only prayer used in practically the whole of the Western Church. With the missionary expansion beginning in the sixteenth century, the Roman Canon was carried all over the world and continued as the only eucharistic prayer in use in the Roman Rite until 1968 when three new eucharistic prayers were introduced. These three new prayers are in fact something of an amalgam, gathering into one format aspects which are peculiar to the Roman Canon, the Gallican tradition, and the Antioch tradition.[22]

It will be useful here to outline the main structure and the principal elements of the Christian eucharistic prayer, as it is found in the four prayers that are now in use. This attempt to analyse the different sections of the prayer should not lead one to forget its internal unity. There is an internal movement or rhythm by which the prayer advances naturally from one point to another, from the introductory dialogue into the preface, and on to the final *Amen*. This division into parts for the sake of analysis must not allow us to forget that the whole prayer is one of thanksgiving and praise, the whole prayer is consecratory, where memorial and intercession intertwine and overlap bringing out different aspects of God's presence in our midst.

iii) *Structure and content*

    a) Introductory dialogue.
    b) Preface.
    c) Sanctus.
    d) Transition.
    e) Invocation of the Holy Spirit upon the gifts.
    f) Institution narrative.

[22] There is not space to follow up this point here, but the reader who wants to go further would do well to read: Cipriano Vagaggini, *The Canon of the Mass and Liturgical Reform,* Geoffrey Chapman, London 1967; Louis Bouyer, *The Eucharist,* University of Notre Dame Press, 1968; Lucien Deiss, *Early Sources of the Liturgy,* Geoffrey Chapman, London 1967; A. Hünggi -I. Pahl, Spicilegium Friburgense, *Prex Eucharistia, Textus e variis liturgiis antiquioribus selecti,* Editions Universitaires, Fribourg 1968.

g) Memorial acclamation.
h) Sacrificial memorial.
i) Invocation of the Holy Spirit upon the community.
j) Intercessions for the Church and the world.
k) Concluding doxology.

a) *Introductory dialogue:* 'Let us give thanks'—from the very outset of the prayer, the predominant note is struck. The offering is to be made in a spirit of gratitude. But it is an invitation, and we see that this is a prayer which the priest makes in the name of the whole community. It is a prayer in which the community takes part, and as the celebrant launches forward into the prayer he goes with the assent and backing of the entire assembly. In the Sanctus, the memorial acclamation and the final *Amen,* the assembly expresses its acceptance and ratification of what he is saying on its behalf and unites itself in heart and mind with Christ, in whose name the celebrant is presiding.

b) *The Preface:* The preface opens in the style of the Jewish blessing invoking the name of God, praising and thanking him for the work of creation, for all the good things he has given us, for all that he is in himself. In this Christian prayer however there is a fundamental difference. God is addressed as Father, the Father revealed to us through his Son. The Christian's response is one of love and gratitude for the love the Father has shown us in his incarnate Son, and the prayer expresses a keen awareness of God's presence and a complete trust in his love for us.
We spoke earlier of the way the Jewish prayer of blessing moved from praise and thanksgiving to memorial and on into a prayer of petition or intercession. This threefold movement is also found in the Christian eucharistic prayer, but the way it develops reflects the way in which the persons of the Trinity have revealed themselves in the course of history.[23] The prayer is addressed in thanksgiving to the Father: it was his initiative, his love, that brought creation into being and it was he who sent his Son to renew this creation. The heart of the prayer is the sacrificial memorial, the memorial of all that the mystery of the incarnate Son of God means to us. But as the Son came to

[23] Louis Ligier, 'De la Cène de Jesus à l'Anaphore de l'Eglise', *La Maison Dieu,* 87 (1966) p. 48.

give us his Spirit, so the prayer moves on to the request that Christ's Spirit may penetrate our lives, the life of the whole Church, the Church in the world. In the final doxology we see the ultimate climax to this mystery in the glory and honour given to the Father through Christ and in the unity of the Spirit.

This preface then, addressed to the Father, is essentially a hymn of rejoicing. Unlike the Eastern Churches, however, the Roman Rite varies this first part of the eucharistic prayer in accordance with the feast being celebrated. This gives considerable flexibility to the prayer and means that particular emphasis can be given to the aspect of man's salvation which is being celebrated. This flexibility has been increased recently by the restoration of eight new prefaces in 1968,[24] and seventy more new prefaces in 1969. Imaginative use of this wealth of prefaces will help to keep the different aspects of the mystery of Christ before our minds. In each case the recalling of the mystery being celebrated leads back into praise and rejoicing: 'And so, with all the multitude of angels in the heavenly courts, we proclaim your glory as we join with their unending hymn. . . .'

c) *The Sanctus:* The Sanctus is the unending hymn to which the last line of our last paragraph refers. An amalgam of the angels' song of praise (Is 6:3) and the crowd's greeting to Our Lord as he entered Jerusalem before his passion (Mt 21:9; Ps 118:26), the Sanctus had become a regular feature of the eucharistic prayer by the fourth century, and has remained so ever since. It comes as a natural response to all that has been proclaimed in the preface, and is of its nature something in which the whole assembly joins in singing.

d) *Transition:* History has shown many ways of linking the Sanctus with the rest of the prayer. In the Gallican tradition, it was done by a prayer called the Vere Sanctus or Post Sanctus, and this is in evidence in the second and third of our eucharistic prayers. By developing the ideas of the Sanctus and relating them to what is to follow, it provides a necessary link and binds the different parts of the prayer together. The Roman Canon and the fourth eucharistic prayer however are clear examples that there are other ways in which the prayer can develop;

[24] Cf Henry Ashworth, 'The New Prefaces', *Clergy Review,* November 1968, pp. 839–60.

a) one has prayers of intercession and a commemoration of the saints,
b) and the other contains a presentation of the history of salvation.

e) *Invocation of the Holy Spirit upon the gifts:* The feature common to all four eucharistic prayers is the prayer before the narrative of the institution of the eucharist that God might consecrate the gifts of bread and wine. In all three of the new prayers, this prayer is a direct request to the Father to send his sanctifying Spirit upon the gifts : 'Let your Spirit come upon these gifts to make them holy, so that they may become for us the Body and Blood of Our Lord Jesus Christ'.

This invocation of the Holy Spirit is connected with the invocation after the words of institution which is a prayer for those who communicate in the gifts. The work of 'sanctifying' the gifts is also the work of him who sanctifies those who share in them, and in many of the Eastern eucharistic prayers these two invocations are bound into one and found after the institution account. The expression 'for us' is obviously not to be taken in a subjective sense, but in the sense that the Body and Blood of Our Lord are objectively present 'on our account', namely as gifts to us through which we are able to unite ourselves to Our Lord in his self-offering to the Father.

It is at this point that we can see how the presentation of gifts is linked with the eucharistic prayer which is said over these gifts.

'The eucharistic gifts of bread and wine are fundamentally (and, yes, ontologically) transformed in their significance or finality precisely because they already are gifts which man receives with gratitude, because they are seen by him already as signs of the Creator's concern for man. This is why the eucharistic anaphora grew so naturally out of the blessing spoken over the bread and cup at the Jewish meal. The Christian faith of the eucharistic assembly, embodied in that act of praise which is the eucharistic prayer, transposes this significance to a higher level so that these elements of bread and wine relate to man in an entirely new way, no longer merely as gifts of the creator but as the saviour's gift of his own flesh and blood unto eternal life.'[25]

[25] Robert J. Ledogar, *art. cit.,* p. 594.

To avoid misunderstanding, we must state the nature of the faith referred to here:

'This faith is not just the faith of the individual participant; it is the faith of the whole Church as shared in by the assembled members of the community. "It is in the Church's sacramental confession of faith," says Schillebeeckx, "that the risen Christ can make an earthly element or human action into a sacramentally visible manifestation of his heavenly act of salvation".'[26]

God's Spirit, who 'hovered over the waters' as Genesis describes creation, is always at work in creation. 'All life, all holiness comes from you, through your Son, Jesus Christ our Lord, by the working of the Holy Spirit', as the third eucharistic prayer says. It is this same Spirit who from age to age gathers a people to the Father 'so that from East to West a perfect offering may be made to the glory of your name'. Conceived in the womb of the virgin Mary by the power of the Holy Spirit, Christ gives to us, his own, this Spirit, his Spirit. If Christians gather together to celebrate the eucharist, it is thanks to the Spirit that they come, and it is through him that they will be united more fully with Christ. The faith we refer to above is the fruit of the Spirit in men's hearts, who draws us together in the Church, and teaches us to praise the Father in the name of Christ, asking that the Words of Christ may be actual and efficacious for us, here and now, as we do what he commanded us to do.

f) *Institution narrative:* It is in this context of thanksgiving and faith, with the community's awareness of the action of the Spirit in their midst, that the celebrant takes the bread and the cup into his hands and repeats Christ's words 'This is my Body which will be given up for you', 'This is the cup of my Blood that will be shed for you'. What is narrated and said is actually achieved and done. Christ's presence among us is achieved at a deeper and fuller level. To understand the full significance of this we must consider the part of the prayer that precedes the institution narrative, and above all the sacrificial memorial and intercession which follow it and with which it is inextricably linked by 'Do this in memory of me'.

[26] *Ibid.,* p. 595, quoting E. Schillebeeckx, *Christ the Sacrament of the Encounter with God,* New York 1963, p. 99.

g) *Memorial acclamation:* The acclamation after the words of institution—a feature in common with many of the eucharistic prayers of the past—does not break the connection with the sacrificial memorial. Quite apart from helping people to refocus their attention and participate more actively in the prayer, it makes a good introduction to the memorial. The English translation is very helpful here. 'Let us proclaim the mystery of faith' —what else is the mystery at this point if not Christ's presence? 'The mystery of Christ is among you, your hope of glory' (Col 1 :27).

This phrase 'mystery of faith' with which the celebrant invites the people's acclamation, brings to mind the understanding of the eucharist as the proclamation of God's presence. This hymn of praise and thanksgiving, which is the eucharistic prayer, is itself a statement of the central mystery of our faith : God's saving action in and through Christ. It is not only a statement of what God has done in the past, but a proclamation of God's saving presence in this particular celebration of the eucharist and in the world in which we live and move. This proclamation of God's presence in our lives demands the response of faith, a faith which penetrates and determines our own existence. This faith is expressed in the acclamation itself : 'Christ has died. Christ is risen. Christ will come again'.

We can be thankful to the International Committee for English in the Liturgy (ICEL), not only because their translation here underlines the aspect of proclamation, but also because the fact that the eucharistic prayers have to be suitable for public proclamation has been a guiding principle in their translation work.

h) *Sacrificial memorial:* The words of this acclamation take us into the heart of the eucharistic prayer, because in the sacramental presence of Christ among his own it is precisely the full mystery of Christ that is present—the objective memorial of the mystery of the incarnation of the Son of God who passed from death to life that we might have life. This 'memorial' is not something subjective, as if it were a thing to which we turned our minds but had no present reality. We have already seen that the Jews celebrating the pasch had an awareness of the continuing effectiveness of God's action among them. The commemoration of the covenant and of God's saving acts of the past were under-

stood as involving a renewal of God's saving action for those
sharing in the paschal meal.

'The recalling of the Exodus event in the passover feast has
the same effect as calling on the divine name (which equals
personality, power of God) in sacrifice (Gen 12 :8), which
entails a coming, a presence, and a blessing : "in every place
where I cause my name to be remembered, I will come to you
and bless you".'[27]

Moreover it was seen as a pledge of the definitive covenant
that was to come.]

This recalling—but not repeating—of the past event, in such
a way that through words and symbols the efficacy of that event
was, by God's power, realized for those taking part in the rite, is
taken up in the Christian eucharist, and endowed with a reality
and fullness of presence that completely surpasses the Pasch of the
past. The 'symbol' of the presence of Christ's saving act is the
actual presence of the risen Christ.

This memorial is a *sacrificial memorial* : an act in which the
Church offers to the Father the memorial of Christ's saving work.
Eucharistic Prayer II, puts it very simply :

'In memory of his death and resurrection, we offer you,
Father, this lifegiving bread, this saving cup'

and this is explicitated by Prayer IV :

'Father, we now celebrate this memorial of our redemption.
We recall Christ's death, his descent among the dead, his resurrection, and his ascension to your right hand; and, looking
forward to his coming in glory, we offer you his Body and
Blood, the acceptable sacrifice which brings salvation to the
whole world.'

The Mass then is truly a sacrifice. The difference between the
Mass understood as an objective memorial, a sacrifice which the
Church offers, rather than a merely subjective recalling of a
past event is clear from what has been said above. The term
'memorial' is used because it has been the language used by
the liturgy itself over the centuries and because it helps us to

---

[27] Edward J. Kilmartin, *The Eucharist in the Primitive Church,* Engle-
wood Cliffs, N.J. 1965, p. 72.

understand the nature of the Mass in terms of its origins in Judaism and in the Lord's Last Supper. But continuing confusion and misunderstanding on this point require that one should be unequivocally clear. Some have remarked that the stress on the eucharistic prayers as a prayer of praise and thanksgiving could seem to reduce the Mass to a sacrifice of praise alone. This has not been my intention any more than it was the Church's intention when, over the centuries, she used the words of the Roman Canon which refer to the eucharist as 'this sacrifice of praise'. The sacrifice referred to here is the supreme sacrifice of praise and thanksgiving : the one and unique self-offering of Christ himself to the Father on our behalf. In the words of the Council of Trent : 'There is the same oblation, and the same person who now makes the oblation through the ministry of the priests and who once made an oblation of himself on the cross. Only the manner of offering is different', In his classic *The Mass of the Roman Rite,* Fr Jungmann states this point clearly :

'The Council of Trent was careful to clarify this very phase of the eucharistic mystery. The Council stressed the doctrine that the Mass is not a mere meal nor only a memorial service recalling a sacrifice that had taken place of yore, but is itself a sacrifice possessing its own power of atonement and petition. Christ had offered this sacrifice at the Last Supper and had given his Apostles and their successors the commission to offer it. Indeed he himself makes the offering through their ministry. Thus he left his beloved spouse, the Church, a visible sacrifice. The Mass is therefore a sacrifice which is made by Christ and at the same time by the recipients of his commission; it is the *sacrifice of Christ* and the *sacrifice of the Church'* (pp. 136–7).

It should be pointed out that while, as implied in the texts just quoted, the part played by the ordained priest is a necessary and irreplaceable element in the celebration of the Christian Eucharist, it is the whole of the Church which offers the sacrifice. As art. 11 of *The Constitution of the Church* says, by reason of baptism it is the right and duty of the Christian people 'to offer the divine Victim to God and themselves along with it'.

We can see clearly from this that in making Christ's sacrifice her own, the Church—and in particular *this* assembly—is actively uniting herself to the offering which Christ makes to his Father. It is he in fact who continues to make intercession for us before the Father, and it is only in and through him that our offering is acceptable to the Father. It is in and through him that the Church offers the memorial of his passion, his resurrection, his unique intercession.

i) *The invocation of the Holy Spirit upon the community:* But what is the object of Christ's intercession? What is the point of his death and resurrection? The scriptures give an unequivocal reply : the gift of his sanctifying Spirit. Jesus Christ offered himself to the Father *in order that* his glorified humanity, transformed in the power of the Spirit who was poured out upon him by the Father in his resurrection, might be the source of the life-giving Spirit for men. Uniting ourselves with him in his self-offering, we make his prayer our own—offering this memorial to the Father is in itself a prayer that the Spirit might come. But this prayer, already implicit in the sacrificial memorial, immediately becomes explicit : 'May all of us who share in the Body and Blood of Christ be brought together in unity by the Holy Spirit' (Prayer II).

Our offering of ourselves to Our Lord is achieved and fully expressed by the communion in his Body and Blood, by communion in his sacrifice. This invocation takes the form of a prayer that the Holy Spirit may transform those who communicate in the offering, and so they may enter more fully into the mystery of Christ's death and resurrection which is being celebrated. It is through this integration into the mystery of Christ that our reconciliation with the Father is expressed and achieved, and this is why we often find an accent on *unity* in this prayer :

> 'Lord, look upon this sacrifice which you have given to your Church : and by your Holy Spirit, gather all who share this bread and wine into the one Body of Christ, a living sacrifice of praise' (Prayer IV).

The accent is on the unity of the Body of Christ, the Church. A twofold movement thus becomes apparent in the eucharistic prayer.[28] In the first part the praise and thanksgiving to the Father

---

[28] Max Thurian, 'Théologie des Prières Eucharistiques', *Maison Dieu* 94 (1968) p. 89.

for all he has done leads into a prayer that the Holy Spirit may consecrate the gifts, so that they may become the sacramental Body and Blood of Christ. In the second part, the presence of Christ's sacramental Body leads to the memorial of all God has done, and to a prayer that the Holy Spirit may gather those who share in the gifts into the unity of the Body of Christ, the Church. As we can see, the Church makes the eucharist, and the eucharist makes the Church. It is important to understand here the relationship between the real presence of Our Lord in the eucharist and his real presence as Lord living in the Church. After all, there is ultimately only one real presence of Christ, although this can come about in various ways.[29]

'This is my Body which will be given for you.' In the eucharist what Our Lord gives us is not a thing, a sign of his love, but himself. What the Church gives in response is herself, expressed in the individual case by actually taking part and by communicating in the Body of the Lord. Christ's sacramental presence, then, is ordered towards his presence in his own, in his Church.

'The "Body of the Lord" in the christological sense is the source of the "Body of the Lord" in the ecclesiological sense. Christ's "eucharistic Body" is the community of the two—the reciprocal real presence of Christ and his Church, meaningfully signified sacramentally in the nourishing of the "Body that is the Church" by Christ's Body.'[30]

Christ's giving of himself to the Church is at the same time an expression of love and self-surrender to the Father, and he expresses his love for the Church by enabling her to share in his loving relationship of self-giving to the Father. The Church responds to this love by willingly uniting herself with, through, and in him in this relationship to the Father. But just as his love for the Father is expressed in his love for us, so too if the Church shares in his relationship with the Father she will be moved by his Spirit to a paternal love and service among men. Then truly will there be worship 'in spirit and truth'.

[29] Edward Schillebeeckx, *The Eucharist*, Sheed and Ward, London 1968, p. 138.
[30] *Ibid.,* p. 140.

j) *The intercessions and commemoration of the saints:* We can see then why this invocation of the Spirit has been called 'a prayer-statement of assimilation or integration with God above all things and with our neighbour as ourselves' and 'how there naturally comes to be allied with this prayer-statement inter-cessory prayer for members of the community—our brethren through Christ in the Spirit, and commemoration of the saints, our brethren now in complete unity in the bosom of the Father'.[31]

These intercessions in fact are a natural development upon the prayer that the Holy Spirit might come upon the community. In the Roman Canon they are found both before and after the institution narrative but in the three new prayers they assume a more logical place after the second invocation of the Holy Spirit. It is the Holy Spirit who gathers us together and enables us to offer ourselves with Christ. This offering is expressed in our com-mitment to the world as Christians and the intercessions gradually open out from the prayer for all the members of the Church to the world at large.

> 'Remember those who take part in this offering, those here present and all your people, and all who seek you with a sincere heart. Remember those who have died in the peace of Christ, and all the dead whose faith is known to you alone.'

There is no reason at all why there should not be a pause of silence at this point in the new eucharistic prayers, as there is in the Roman Canon, in which people call to mind the living and the dead for whom they wish especially to pray. The objec-tive memorial of the mystery of Christ is, we have said, our sacrifice, and this is in itself an invocation of the Holy Spirit upon those communicating in the sacrifice, an invocation which in itself contains our prayer for all the needs of man :

> 'Lord, may this sacrifice, which has made our peace with you, advance the peace and salvation of all the world' (Prayer III).

In all four prayers there is a request which brings us face to face with the ultimate finality of the eucharist : 'Enable us to share in the inheritance of your saints, with Mary, the virgin mother of God : with the apostles, the martyrs and all your

[31] Aidan Kavanagh, 'Thoughts on the Roman Anaphora,' *Worship* 39 (November 1965) p. 529.

saints.' Yes, the kingdom of God is amongst us through the presence of Christ and his vivifying Spirit, but it has not yet been revealed in its fullness. It is to that that our eyes turn in the prayer, for the present celebration of the eucharist is an anticipation and preparation for the time when 'he will come again'. Far from distracting us from present reality as 'an opium of the people' our confidence for the future is all the more reason for working for the renewal of all things in Christ here and now. But there is a sobering realism in Christianity : Christ never promised that the way to resurrection was other than the cross.

In all that we have said of the eucharist and the eucharistic prayer, Mary stands before us as an object lesson in what it actually means : her acceptance of Christ's gift of himself, complete reciprocity of the offering of herself together with him to the Father and in the loving service of her fellow men, her receiving in return the fullness of God's love in the gift of his Spirit—in all of this she is the symbol and exemplar of both the Church and the individual Christian. The working out of the eucharistic mystery in her did not occur in some sort of ideal world far removed from our own : her son was born in a cattle-shed; as refugees in Egypt she and her husband had to live by their wits, taking each day as it came; as the incident in the temple showed, bringing up their boy had much the same difficulties as it does for other parents; later her son met misunderstandings, mistrust, and even hatred from those who should have been the first to show sympathy and a response; and they spat on her son, nailing him to pieces of wood amid the mounds of rubble outside the city. The years which followed were not much easier, as her son's followers were harried and persecuted as enemies of true religion and a danger to the established political and religious order. In all of this Mary's loving faith did not falter, she did not come out of it bitter, cynical, or full of self-pity. Her faith deepened and matured in love. It expressed itself in her whole life—'eternal life is this : to know you, the only true God, and Jesus Christ whom you have sent' (Jn 17 :3). There are ways and ways of knowing.

There are others who have followed the same path as Mary. I remember that elderly lady sitting one Sunday in the fifth row from the front. She was holding a rosary loosely in her lap and patiently listening to the young and eager preacher speaking about the Mass. She had lived through two world wars and the depression. She had experienced, in her own family, the cycle of birth, marriage and death. Her mind and heart had been with Christ throughout—and although she had not studied the texts or burrowed among the tomes of *Wissenschaft* as had the young preacher, it may be that she *knew* in a way that he had hardly begun to know. There are others, men and women of different ages and experience in the congregation, who have begun to know as she does. Their prayer, like Mary's, like the Church's prayer, could well be in the words of the psalmist: 'What is heaven to me without you? Where am I on earth if you are not there? Though my body is broken down, though my heart dies, you are my Rock, my God, the future that waits for me.'[32] This expresses a communion with God which will only be fully realized when Christ comes again, but of which the eucharist is an anticipation and preparation, a 'knowledge' to which all our pastoral efforts are directed.

k) *Concluding doxology:* The conclusion of the eucharistic prayer is always a doxology: a prayer giving praise and adoration to God. United in the Holy Spirit, this particular assembly, and, indeed, the whole Church offers its praise and thanksgiving to the Father through Christ. Just as this is taken up into Christ's own gift of himself to the Father, so too Christ offers the whole of creation to his Father—an offering symbolized and achieved in the eucharist by the power of the Spirit.

In the final *Amen,* the congregation confirms and ratifies what has been proclaimed in its name.

iv. *The four eucharistic prayers*

The structure of the eucharistic prayer, as outlined above, is found in each of our four eucharistic prayers. But a study of the eucharistic prayers of the past would quickly show that the format or pattern does not have to be exactly the same as the one described above. The same basic ingredients can be combined in a great variety of ways. There is no reason why eucharistic prayers of the future, originating for example in Ceylon or Africa,

[32] Cf *Fifty Psalms: An Attempt at a New Translation*, Burns & Oates London 1968, p. 73.

should have to follow exactly the same format. Why then was it followed in the three new eucharistic prayers? The reasons were twofold : on the one hand there was a desire to maintain the identity of the Roman Rite, and on the other the pastoral motive that this uniformity would facilitate the people's participation and help them to see the continuity between the new and the old.

The Roman Canon has been retained as Eucharistic Prayer I. In use for almost fifteen hundred years in the Roman rite, it has stood the test of time well and has been an abundant source of life and light for many. One of its principal merits is the theology it contains of the offering of the gifts. The rich collection of prefaces in the Roman tradition, and the variable Communicantes and Hanc igiturs also afford a certain flexibility and variety. The emphasis in the text on the fellowship of those at Mass with the apostles, the martyrs and all the saints, highlights the relationship between 'this altar' and 'the altar in heaven', where the Lamb sacrificed on Calvary continually intercedes on our behalf.

Eucharistic Prayer II is based on one of the most ancient eucharistic prayers that we possess—that of Hippolytus' *Apostolic Tradition*. It is characterized by simplicity and clarity. Its theme is Christ, and the preface is a hymn of thanksgiving to the Father for all that his Son is, and for all that his Son has done for us. With remarkable brevity, it delineates our Lord's work of gathering for his Father a new people through his death and resurrection. In describing our Lord's offering of himself, the text underlines the freedom with which he made this sacrifice : 'For our sake he opened his arms on the cross', and 'Before he was given up to death, a death he freely accepted', and his own words 'this is my Body which will be given up for you'. It is thus to the person of Christ and to his free gift of himself for us that this prayer takes us, rather than to an abstract philosophy or system of ideas. In this the nature of the eucharistic prayer as a statement, a grateful acknowledgement, of Christ's saving presence is clearly seen.

Eucharistic Prayer III does not have a preface of its own but can be used with any of the prefaces now available. These prefaces of the Roman tradition, often drawing on the Pauline Epistles for their inspiration, can be of great assistance in helping bring out aspects of the feast or liturgical season being celebrated. Perhaps the most significant feature of this prayer, and one of lasting importance, is that it is not just an adaptation of an ancient eucharistic prayer, but a new composition. It retains the basic structure of the Roman Canon while incorporating elements of the Gallican tradition, so that the word 'new' should not be over-emphasized. But the fact remains that the Church has not hesitated to adopt for official use a prayer which has been compiled in our own time. Among the points which stand out in this prayer are the emphasis it gives to the role of the Spirit in the eucharist, and the eucharist as a sacrifice. The two are closely linked. It is the Spirit who gathers the Christian community to make the 'perfect offering' to the Father. It is the Spirit who sanctifies and transforms the gifts and who sanctifies those who share in them, so that by sharing in the eucharistic Body of Christ we become the Body of Christ, temple of his Spirit. In this way, says the prayer, we become 'an everlasting gift to God'. The fruit of sharing in Christ's sacrifice is not only 'our peace with God' but the advancement of the peace and salvation of all the world', and so the prayer opens out to the needs of all men.

Eucharistic Prayer IV is perhaps the most popular of the new eucharistic prayers. Yet it is the one which moves furthest away from the Roman tradition. By the way it outlines the whole economy of salvation it places itself firmly in the Antioch tradition, which, as we saw earlier, is probably linked in an especial way with the second of the three blessings at the end of the paschal meal. Fr Joseph Gelineau has pointed out that the whole of the first half of the prayer is a thanksgiving to God the Father: a) for all that he is in himself; b) for creation, especially that of man, and, after the fall, for the beginnings of the work of salvation; c) for the mission of his only Son who was made man, was revealed as the Messiah, who died and rose again; d) for the mission of the Spirit in the Church, who continues the work of the saviour, particularly through the sharing in Christ's paschal mystery in the Church's sacramental life. The second half of the prayer is basically the same as in the other two new eucharistic prayers, although the order of intercessions differs slightly in each of them. The way the intercessions are presented in these prayers shows that the history of salvation is achieved in the glory of God's presence in heaven.

In the norms given for their use it was indicated that the first
and third prayers were especially well suited for use on Sundays.
As pointed out already, this is in order to ensure that the prefaces
of the Roman tradition are not abandoned, but it does not mean
that the second and fourth prayers cannot be used on Sundays.
The only time these last *cannot* be used is when the preface is
strictly proper, namely on the feast day to which it belongs or
during the octave of that feast (*Notitiae*, 47, July-August 1969,
p. 323). Regarding the use of the formula for a dead person
which may be inserted into the second and third eucharistic
prayers, the new Order of the Mass makes it clear *when* these
can be used (no. 322b), namely, they can be used whenever the
Mass is celebrated for a dead person or whenever particular
memory of this person is made. The purpose of this is to make
the recommendation of no. 316 of the General Instruction easier
to carry out, where it refers to the *moderate* use of requiem
Masses (*Notitiae*, op. cit., p. 325).

iv) *Actual celebration of the eucharistic prayer*

Speaking and singing: In trying to find how and where a
thing is to be done, it is worth considering *what* we are trying
to do and *why* it is done. It is useful to remember this when
interpreting the Order of the Mass with the People, since one
can often see what the General Instruction accompanying it has
to say, and the Instruction is concerned with *what* the thing
means and *why* it is to be done. A case in point is where the
Order says: 'In all Masses it is permitted for the celebrating
priest to say the eucharistic prayer out loud if this seems suitable'
(OMP, no. 28). At the end of an exposition of the nature of the
eucharistic prayer, the Instruction says 'the eucharistic prayer
demands that all should listen to it with reverence and in silence,
and should take part in it through the acclamations'. From all
that we have said above about the nature of this prayer, this
makes good sense. It is a public prayer in the name of the whole
assembly, and it is therefore natural that it should be out loud
and understood by all present.

The parts which can be sung are: the introductory dialogue
and preface, the Sanctus, the memorial acclamation, the doxology
and the Amen. In the Roman Canon, the part of the prayer from

the first invocation (Quam oblationem) through to the second invocation (Supplices) can be sung, and in the other eucharistic prayers, the Institution narrative and the memorial. The parts that most demand singing are the Sanctus, the memorial acclamation and the final Amen.

'The great Amen at the end of the eucharistic prayer requires care. It is difficult to make an enthusiastic acclamation out of this single two-syllable word. Composers should feel free to repeat it several times or to explicate its many meanings when setting it to music.'[33]

New rubrics: The prayer begins after the short pause following the prayer over the gifts. The introductory dialogue should be fresh and vigorous in order to give impetus to the prayer that is to follow. The rubrics of the new Order indicate that the celebrant extends his hands as he greets the people: 'The Lord be with you', raises his extended hands a little as he says 'Lift up your hearts', and keeps them raised and extended until he joins his hands at the beginning of the Sanctus. Clearly, these rubrics are not concerned with any mathematical precision but aim at ensuring that the gestures help express the content of the words they accompany. Words and gestures are expressing the same reality, and should flow into one another naturally.

The preface, as a hymn/prayer of praise and thanksgiving, should obviously be said in a way which expresses this and be neither rattled off at top speed nor said like a dirge. The last lines of the preface are an introduction to the Sanctus. The celebrant then sings or recites the Sanctus with the congregation, and does not continue with the prayer until the Sanctus is over:

'The nature of the "presidential" parts of the Mass demands that they should be proclaimed clearly and loudly, and that all should listen with attention. While the priest says them there should be no other prayers or singing, and the organ and other musical instruments should be silent' (GI, 12).

After the Sanctus the priest continues, extending his hands again in the attitude of prayer. If people kneel at this point, a few moments' pause will mean that the first words are not drowned

[33] Statement of Music, Advisory Board to U.S. Bishops, *op. cit.*

by the rattle of benches. The priest's hands remain extended until
the prayer or invocation of God's action for the consecration of
the gifts. During this prayer the priest extends his hands over the
gifts in the same way that a bishop extends his hands over an
ordinand in the rite of ordination : the meaning of this imposition
is the same in each case, namely the prayer for the sanctifying
action of God's Spirit upon this person of these gifts. This means
that in the Roman Canon this extending of the hands over the
gifts is now during the Quam oblationem (which is the
prayer for the consecration of the gifts in the Roman Canon)
and not during the Hanc igitur.

When we come to the words of institution there is obviously
a difference in the type of action demanded of the celebrant
when he is celebrating on an altar facing the people and when
he celebrates facing away from the people. In both cases 'the
words of the Lord are to be pronounced clearly and distinctly
as the nature of these words demands' (OMP, 91). But particularly when facing the people, the gestures must be well co-
ordinated with the words themselves. As the celebrant says 'Take
this, all of you, and eat it : this is my Body which will be given
up for you', it is a natural gesture to lift the bread up and towards
the people. The words 'This is my Body' are an affirmation of
fact, and are understood in the light of the invocation of the Holy
Spirit upon the gifts which has gone before; but they are also
demonstrative—the gestures should express this and draw the
congregation's visual and aural attention at the same moment.[34]
The same goes for the gestures accompanying the words over the
chalice. This is clearly a point where the congregation must have
easy sight and sound, and not have to strain their senses to see
and hear. The genuflection the priest makes—first after the words
over the bread, and secondly after the words over the wine—will
inevitably reflect something of his attitude to the mystery that is
being celebrated, and this has an effect on the congregation's
attitude.

The celebrant invites the congregation to join him in the
acclamation, and after the acclamation he extends his hands as
before and proclaims the sacrificial memorial.

A point to be noticed is that in the three new eucharistic
prayers the celebrant no longer bows over the altar during the

<hr>

[34] Cf Raymond Clarke, *op. cit.*, p. 68–9.

invocation of the Holy Spirit upon the community. This is in order to avoid the difficulties which arise with this gesture when trying to read a text that may not be too familiar, and at the same time speak in such a way that all can hear.

⌈ In concelebrated Masses the concelebrants twice extend their hands—at the prayer for the consecration of the gifts, before the institution narrative ('with hands extended over the offerings', OMP, 174), and during the words of institution themselves ('with the right hand extended over the bread and wine', OMP, 174). The second of these gestures is optional, but two points should be noted. First, it is better if all the concelebrants agree to make or not to make the second gesture, and to do it in the same way if they do make it; second, in both cases the gesture is in the nature of an invocation of God's action (as in the ordination rite) and not merely a 'pointing' gesture, and therefore should be made in the same way in both cases.[35] The Instruction makes another pertinent remark about concelebration :

> 'the parts which are to be said by all the concelebrants to-gether are to be said in such a way that the voices of the concelebrants are lowered and the voice of the principal cele-brant is heard. In this way the text will be more easily under-stood by the people' (GI, 170). ⌋

The rubric referring to the gestures during the concluding doxology has been modified. It is a good example of the laconic style of the new rubrics : 'He takes the paten with the host and the chalice, and lifts them both' (OMP, 71, 79, 86, 95). The simplest way of doing this is to take the paten which contains the consecrated bread in one hand, the chalice in the other, and lift them both to about face or shoulder height—but not directly in front of the face, since the gesture is accompanying words which sum up the whole of the eucharistic prayer : we are offering our sacrifice of praise and thanksgiving, Christ's own supreme and unique sacrifice, through him, with him and in him, and indeed thanks to him, in the unity of the Holy Spirit to the Father whose love is the origin of all things, and to whom his creation responds.

[35] Cipriano Vagaggini, 'L'extension de la main au moment de la conse-cration: geste indicatif ou épiclétique', *Paroisse et liturgie,* 1 (1969) pp. 46–53.

If there is a deacon he holds the chalice during the doxology, and the priest holds the paten. Both priest and deacon should continue to hold up the paten and chalice until the end of the people's *Amen*. There is no longer a genuflection at this point, but a few moments' pause before going on to the Lord's prayer would seem advisable.

4. THE COMMUNION RITE

i) *Significance*

As we saw above, we enter most fully into the sacrifice of Christ through communion in his sacrifice. Communion expresses not only the community's faith in Christ, and desires for union with him, but also the desire to share in the worship and love he has towards his Father and towards his fellow-men. This is expressed primarily in a prayer that communion in Christ's sacramental body may bring a fuller unity, communion, in Christ's Body, the Church. The invocation of the Holy Spirit upon the community in the eucharistic prayer has precisely that object : 'Grant that we who are nourished by his Body and Blood may be filled with his Holy Spirit, and become one body, one spirit in Christ'. The Holy Spirit is the bond of unity with the 'churches' so that together they form the one Church of Christ. *The Constitution on the Church* beautifully expresses the significance of the eating of Christ's Body and the drinking of his Blood in this context :

'The Church of Christ is truly present in all legitimate congregations of the faithful which, united with their pastors, are themselves called churches in the New Testament. For in their own locality these are the new people called by God, in the Holy Spirit, and in much fullness (cf I Th 1 :5). In them the faithful are gathered together by the preaching of the gospel of Christ, and the mystery of the Lord's supper is celebrated, "that by the flesh and blood of the Lord's body the whole brotherhood may be joined together".

'In any community existing around an altar, under the sacred ministry of the bishop, there is manifested a symbol of that charity and "unity of the Mystical Body without which there can be no salvation". In these communities, though frequently small and poor, or living far from any other, Christ is present. By virtue of him the one, holy, catholic, and apostolic Church gathers together. For "the partaking of the Body and Blood of Christ does nothing other than transform us into that which we consume" ' (art. 26).

This last phrase might also be translated as 'become what we are,' and in a way this sums up the whole of the Christian life, and it certainly sums up the significance of eucharistic communion. Entering into the death and resurrection of Christ through faith and baptism (Rom 6 : 2–4; Gal 3 : 26), we enter more fully into this mystery when we receive his Body and Blood with faith. It is Christ's Spirit who draws us into this union with him. 'In one Spirit, we were all baptized, Jews and Greek, slaves as well as citizens, and one Spirit was given us all to drink' (1 Cor 12 : 13). This same Spirit impels and moves us actually to live as sons and daughters of the Father, as brothers and sisters of Christ, seeking to be 'dead to sin, but alive for God in Christ Jesus' (Rom 6 : 11)—becoming what we are! St Paul develops this at length (cf Rom 8; Gal 5 : 16–26), but sums it up simply 'Since the Spirit is our life, let us be directed by the Spirit' (Gal 5 : 26). Far from being empty moralizing, this is the heart of Christian life. The love, care, concern and action which is shown in commitment at the individual and social level, according to differing demands of time and place, are its living and ineradicable expression.

The celebration of this part of the eucharist must aim at bringing out the riches it contains, helping all who take part to grasp and enter into what is being signified. This means that the celebration must show forth in signs that the first fruit of the eucharist is the unity of the Body of Christ, Christians loving Christ through loving one another,[36] human love becoming the sacrament of divine love. The reform has sought to put these elements in clearer relief.

It emphasizes the Lord's prayer, the 'kiss' or gesture of peace with one another, and the breaking of bread—all of which stress the aspect of unity and mutual love. In the communion it has sought to encourage the communion of all taking part; to underline the taking part in *this* sacrifice by taking communion with bread consecrated at that Mass; to try and develop an under-

[36] Statement of Music Advisory Board to the U.S. Bishops, *op. cit.*

standing of communion as really eating by making the bread ③
actually look like bread; to bring out the fullness of sign by
encouraging communion under both kinds, to develop an appre- ④
ciation of communion by the period of silent prayer or songs of
thanksgiving and praise which follow it.

The history of the communion rite is, like that of the prepara-   *HISTORY.*
tion of the gifts, a complex one.[37] Originally, the act of com- ①
munion came at the end of the eucharistic blessing or prayer, but
by the fourth century the communion is accompanied by prayers, ②
the Our Father and the postcommunion standing out as the
most important among them.

> 'At the time of Pope Gregory I (d.604) the general pattern
> for the communion rite was something like this : Pater noster,
> breaking of bread, kiss of peace, reception of communion under
> both species, singing of a psalm during the communion pro-
> cession, postcommunion, dismissal.'[38]

This passage also outlines the way the communion rite has been
reformed. There was a great deal of discussion—in the groups
working on the Mass reform—as to where the breaking of the
bread was to be placed. Some wanted to place it immediately
after the eucharistic prayer—'he took and broke the bread',
while others wanted to relate it closely to communion itself—'he
broke it and gave it to his disciples'. The position in the Mass of
the rite of peace was discussed, and finally both the breaking of
the bread and the rite of peace were so placed as hardly to dis-
turb the former order of the Mass at this point. We shall now
take each part of the communion rite in turn, presenting the
significance of each part and offering suggestions for the rite's
celebration.

ii) *Actual celebration*

The communion rite falls easily into three parts. *The first part,*
a preparation for communion, emphasizes the unity, peace and
love which must characterize those who receive Christ's Body,
and consists of the Lord's prayer, the kiss of peace and the breaking
of the bread. *The second part* is the actual distribution of com-

---

[37] For a full treatment of this, cf Joseph Jungmann, *op. cit.*, pp. 461–531.
[38] Johannes Bauer, *op. cit.*, p. 106.

munion. *The third part* is the thanksgiving together with the prayer after communion, or postcommunion, which closes the n e and sums up its meaning much in the same way as the prayer over the gifts earlier on in the Mass sums up the significance of the presentation of gifts.

FIRST PART : *Preparation for Communion*

a)   *The Lord's prayer*

'Here we ask for our daily bread. This is given to Christians in the Body of Christ above all. We ask for purification from our sins so that the holy things may be given to holy people' (GI, 56).

This reference to 'daily bread' is almost certainly one of the principal reasons why this prayer has been included as a preparation for communion in all the liturgies of the Church since the fourth century. This extension of the idea of bread as applying also to the eucharistic bread recurs many times in the writings of the Fathers. It is probable that the Our Father was also used in domestic ceremonies, namely when Christians took communion from the eucharistic bread they had brought home from the Sunday celebration to use during the week.

The 'Let us pray' which used to introduce this section has now been dropped. For one thing, the prayer *par excellence* has only just taken place so it is not as if the community has not been praying. But, more important, by putting it under the invitation to prayer which came with the 'Let us give thanks', the Our Father is linked more closely with the eucharistic prayer without becoming part of it and without ceasing to be a prayer in direct preparation for communion. In a way it sums up the eucharistic prayer—'blessed' or 'hallowed' 'be your name', expressing the prayer of praise and thanksgiving which has gone before, and 'thy kingdom come' succinctly expressing the content of the invocation of the Holy Spirit upon the gifts and upon the community. The prayer that the Father's will be done indicates the community's desire to be united, through communion, in heart and mind with Christ in his sacrifice to the Father.[39] As the

---

[39] Joseph Jungmann, *op. cit.*, p. 464.

introduction to the Lord's prayer makes clear, it is in union with Christ that we are able to say 'our' Father.

The reference in the text of the General Instruction 'holy things for the holy' is an acclamation still used in the Byzantine rite. Fundamentally it refers to the 'holiness' of the baptized, who alone may receive the holy things of the eucharist. It is a call to recognize the holiness of these eucharistic gifts. It is not to be taken in a Jansenistic sense as if communion was only for the 'perfect', for those who have 'arrived'. Communion is not given to us because of anything we can offer God, but as a free gift of the Father in order that we may be transformed in the sanctifying action of Christ's Spirit—just as Christ came to save sinners not the just!

'Embolism' is a word often used to describe the prayer developing or elaborating the last petition of the Lord's prayer, and which is said by the celebrant alone. Today 'embolism' is more likely to make people think of blood clots than a prayer, and it would be better to find another name. This is a prayer that has existed in almost all the liturgies of the Church developing the prayer to be kept free of Evil and all evils. In the Roman Rite it developed further into a prayer for internal and external peace.

The revision of this text in our rite was carried out against the background of the Roman Canon, and before the new eucharistic prayers had been written. It was felt on the one hand that the list of saints duplicated the commemorations of the Canon, and on the other that a reference to our Lord's second coming, to the eschatological aspect of the eucharist, was lacking in the Roman Rite, and could easily be inserted here after the manner of the Eastern rites. Even with the advent of the new eucharistic prayers, the new arrangement was preferred. The revision is as follows :

> 'Deliver us, Lord, from every evil, and grant us peace in our day. In your mercy keep us free from sin and protect us from all anxiety as we wait in joyful hope for the coming of our Saviour Jesus Christ.'

The line newly inserted into the prayer is taken from Paul's letter to Titus 2 : 13 : 'Waiting in hope for the blessing which will come with the appearing of our Saviour Jesus Christ'. To which the congregation replies : 'For the kingdom and the power and the glory are yours, now and for ever.' This phrase, used by many of the Eastern Churches and separated Western Churches, is found in some of the early manuscripts of Matthew's Gospel as a conclusion to the Lord's prayer. It seems to have been introduced into the text through liturgical usage at a very early date and probably had its origin in the doxologies used in Jewish synagogue worship. It is also found in the Didache. Clearly, it fits the context very well, but given the way in which many people in English-speaking countries were educated to regard this particular acclamation—almost as a symbol of all things Protestant—it will have to be carefully handled when introducing it in the parishes.

It is interesting to note that the reason the acclamation was adopted in the separated Churches of the West, was normally because it was already in use in the Western liturgy. Its use in the Anglican communion for example is almost certainly due to the fact that this acclamation was found in the Sarum Rite, widely used in England before the Reformation.

The Lord's prayer may be either sung or said by all present in the assembly, but care should be taken to ensure that this prayer, which is used by all Christians, is not rattled off out of sheer habit.

As for the rubrics regarding the celebrant—he extends his hands for the Lord's prayer and embolism, joining them again for the people's acclamation.

b) *The rite of peace:* The General Instruction explains that the purpose of the rite of peace is that 'the faithful should implore peace and unity for the Church and for the whole family of mankind, and express the love they have towards one another before sharing in the one Bread' (GI, 56b). The prayer for peace in this rite has been used repeatedly in ecumenical celebrations, and it would be good if this prayer in the Mass was also understood by the faithful as a prayer for the unity of all Christians.

When the acclamation is over, the celebrant, extending his hands in the gesture of public prayer, goes on to say out loud the prayer for peace. After the prayer he says 'the peace of the Lord be with you always' (extending and joining his hands) and then, if desired, either he or a deacon may invite the members of the assembly to exchange a gesture with each other, signifying their spirit of peace and mutual goodwill. The form this gesture takes is left for Episcopal Conferences to decide, according to the character and customs of their own people. The people make this sign of peace—each person to his immediate neighbour—whilst the celebrant makes it to the deacon, minister or server.

While this 'sign of peace' is not obligatory, it is obviously reasonable that people should become accustomed to a consistent pattern in their own parish rather than letting it seem as if it depends on the whim of individual celebrants.

c) *The breaking of the bread:* The breaking of bread, as done by Christ at the Last Supper, was in apostolic times the name given to the entire eucharistic action. This rite does not merely have a partial purpose : it signifies that we who are many are made into one body through communion in the one bread of life, which is Christ (1 Cor 10 : 17).

We are back once again with the practical problem of the type of bread to be used in the celebration, and with the degree to which this sign-value can be realistically maintained when there is a large congregation coming to communion. But there are those who feel that

'by insisting on the use of strange little wafers, unlike anything else we ever see or eat, we drive one more wedge between liturgy and life, fostering irrelevance rather than continuity between them. Tradition at its best is calling us ever more strongly to return to the use of real bread that is really broken, that really speaks to us, really showing us that it is really one bread that we are really sharing. The *fractio* would then assume its integral place in the fourfold action of the Christian eucharistic tradition.'[40]

One natural reaction however is to shrug this off as a practical impossibility—it takes too long, impossible to calculate numbers, etc. If it is not to remain in the realm of pure hypothesis, practical investigation will have to be done by liturgical commissions. Fr Clifford Howell makes some suggestions in this regard :

'The *fractio* can be revitalized in a manner which I have witnessed in Switzerland, in Canada, in Germany and in France on particular occasions. The priest consecrated a large

[40] James McGivern, speaking at the 1966 National Liturgical Week in the U.S.A., quoted by Clifford Howell, 'Reforming the Liturgy: the Communion Rite: II', *Clergy Review*, June 1968, p. 443.

flat loaf of unleavened bread, some six inches by four and
perhaps a quarter of an inch thick. It was made with criss-
crossed grooves on it so that it could be broken easily for
communion. He would consecrate one, two or more of the
loaves according to the number of communicants expected;
he broke them during the Agnus Dei which is, by origin, the
chant to be sung during the breaking of the bread.'[41]

Many will still object that at a normal parish Mass, while
some of the bread may be broken in this way, it is hard to see
how it can be practical with the numbers that come to communion. Personally, I know of no satisfactory answer to that
objection.

In time the desire to achieve a fuller and more real symbolism
may help us to find ways to overcome the practical difficulties,
but there are many who wonder why the Immixtio of part of
the host with the consecrated wine has been retained. The significance and origin of the rite are obscure, and authorities like
Fr Jungmann and Dom Bernard Botte, while offering many possible solutions to the question, admit that none of the explanations
to date are adequate.

Given, however, that it is a rite which is preserved and greatly
honoured in all the Eastern liturgies, and given its almost
universal usage, it was decided to leave the rite intact as in the
Eastern Churches and hope that future scholarship would throw
more light on the subject. The only changes made in the prayer
Haec commixtio were the removal of the word 'consecratio'
which was ambiguous in this context, and the suppression of the
Amen at the end of the prayer.

If the celebrant wishes the significance of the breaking of the
bread to be understood, he must wait a moment after the rite
of peace until the congregation are again giving him their
attention.

He breaks the bread over the paten instead of over the chalice,
and at concelebration the concelebrants can assist in breaking
the bread. The gesture of immixtio consists in placing a particle
of the consecrated bread into the chalice, saying the prayer
silently.

The Lamb of God song accompanies the breaking of the bread

41 Clifford Howell, art. cit., p. 445.

and the immixtio. It may be repeated as many times as is necessary to accompany the action (GI, 56e). However many times it
is sung, the final phrase is always 'grant us peace'. It is sung by
the choir with the people, or by a cantor and the people; if it
is not sung, then it is said out loud (GI, 56f).

SECOND PART: *Communion*

a) *Prayer before communion:* The priest says privately one or
other of the two prayers, Domine Jesu Christe and Perceptio
which were originally, and still remain, prayers by which the
priest prepares for communion. The faithful prepare for communion at the same time in private prayer (GI, 56f).

b) *Presentation of the eucharist bread:*

'Then the priest shows to the faithful the eucharistic bread
which is to be received in communion, and invites them to
share in Christ's own banquet. Using the very words of the
Gospel, he then makes an act of humility, together with the
faithful' (GI, 56g).

The words of John the Baptist declaring the presence of the
Saviour in the world, 'Behold the lamb of God, behold him who
takes away the sins of the world', bring clearly to mind that Christ
is the suffering servant prophesied by Isaiah, and the Paschal
Lamb whose saving sacrifice is even now being celebrated in the
eucharist. These words are followed by: 'Happy are those who
are called to his supper' (Rev 19:9), which underlines our sharing
in Christ's sacrifice through eating and drinking his Body and
Blood. The RSV translates the original image as 'marriage
supper,' a reference to the coming of God's kingdom amongst us,
to his establishing the new covenant, thus bringing men into an
entirely new relationship with God and with their fellow men.
It also calls to mind the marriage between Christ and the Church
which is made manifest every time the eucharist is celebrated,
but which has yet to be fully revealed:

'I saw the holy city, and the new Jerusalem, coming down
from God out of heaven, as beautiful as a bride all dressed for
her husband. Then I heard a loud voice call from the throne,
"You are the city. Here God lives among men. He will make

his home among them; they shall be his people, and he will
be their God; his name is God-with-them. He will wipe away
all tears from their eyes; there will be no more death, and
no more mourning or sadness. The world of the past has
gone" ' (Rev 21 : 2–4).

Aware of the entirely unmerited, gratuitous nature of Christ's
gift of himself, the whole assembly takes up the centurion's words,
and says once together : 'Lord, I am not worthy. . . .'

c) *The communion song:* During the communion of the priest
and the faithful, the communion song is sung. Its purpose is to
express through a union of voices the spiritual unity and joy of
all those communicating, and to make the receiving of the Body
of Christ a genuine expression of brotherhood (GI, 56i). The song
begins when the priest receives communion and is carried on for
whatever time seems reasonable, but 'it should not become
wearisome. If the communion time is of any length, variety
should be sought, e.g. instrumental interlude, period of silence,
choir song, etc.'[42]
The Instruction offers a good number of possibilities for the
song itself : it can be taken from the Roman Gradual (antiphon
alone or with a psalm), or from the Simple Gradual (antiphon
with a psalm), or from among other songs or hymns approved by
the Episcopal Conference. As far as possible, these songs or hymns
should bring out the meaning and implication of eucharistic
communion itself. Worthwhile texts set to good music at this
point can do a great deal to help people see the connection
between the communion they are receiving and their normal life.
The texts can be sung by the choir alone, or by a choir or cantor
with the people. It has been suggested that

'the ideal communion song is the short refrain sung by the
people alternated with cantor or choir. The song can be learned
easily and quickly. The people are not burdened with books,
papers, etc. For the same reason the metric hymn is the least
effective communion song'[43]

unless of course the hymn is well known and people enjoy singing
it. If a hymn is used it must be suitable for this part of the Mass,

[42] Statement of Music Advisory Board to the U.S. Bishops, *op. cit.*
[43] Johannes Bauer, *op. cit.,* p. 116.

and not all the hymns used at eucharistic benediction are suitable as communion hymns.

If there is no singing, the antiphon found in the Missal is recited either by the faithful or by some among them, or by a lector alone. If no one is able to recite the text, the priest says it himself after his own communion, before he distributes communion to the faithful (GI, 56i).

d) *Communion itself:* The formulas for the priest's communion have been simplified : 'Corpus (or Sanguis) Christi custodiat me in vitam aeternum', without the Amen. The private prayers accompanying the priest's communion are no longer put in the Mass text itself, although there will probably be many who have found the prayers valuable and will continue to use them. Nothing has changed with regard to the communion of the faithful, but the Instruction states :

> 'It is earnestly to be desired that the faithful should receive the Body of the Lord from hosts consecrated at the same Mass and that they should share the chalice in those cases already foreseen; it is through these signs that communion is best seen as a participation in the Sacrifice actually being celebrated' (GI, 56h).

First and foremost of course it is desirable that as many as possible of those present should actually come to communion! Considering all we have said about the nature of the Mass, history shows many strange developments with regard to this point. Even as far back as the time of St John Chrysostom, we find pastors complaining that many of the faithful were not communicating on Sundays. The reaction to heresies denying the divinity of Christ led in subsequent centuries to an emphasis on man's unworthiness as he approached the holy table, and the habit of receiving communion steadily declined until in the Middle Ages it was a rare event and almost always preceded by confession. There was at the same time a tendency to separate communion of the faithful from the Mass, and the reforming Council of Trent reacted strongly against both tendencies : 'It is the will of the holy Synod that the faithful, every time they attend the holy sacrifice of the Mass, receive communion, not only spiritual communion, but the real sacramental communion'

(Sess. 2, Can. 6). But the habit of separating the communion of the people from the Mass continued to make progress. In the eighteenth and nineteenth centuries, the celebrant was practically the only one to receive communion during the Mass. The evil and distracting influence of Jansenism further clouded people's understanding of Christ's love, and led many to keep away from communion altogether. The famous devotion to the Sacred Heart was a welcome and very necessary antidote to this and we can only be thankful to St Pius X who, in 1905, urged the practice of frequent communion, stressed its value, and swept away many of the distorted attitudes which had grown up around this subject. But old attitudes die hard, and in some parts of the world confusion on the matter lingers on. Not the least important aspect of this question is that it deeply affects the way people view Christ's incarnation and what Christ means to them.

The Instruction does not lay down any rules as to whether the eucharistic bread is to be received kneeling down or standing up; it is left to local custom and the decision of the Episcopal Conference. When communion is received under both kinds, however, the communicants always stand (GI, 244c).

We have already spoken about communion under both kinds above (pp. 8–9). The cases in which it is permitted at the present time are as follows:

1. to newly baptized adults in the Mass which follows their baptism; to confirmed adults in the Mass of their confirmation; to baptized persons who are received into communion with the Church.

2. to bride and bridegroom in their wedding Mass.

3. to newly ordained in the Mass of their ordination.

4. to abbesses in the Mass of their blessing; to religious sisters in the Mass of their consecration; to professed in the Mass of their first or renewed religious profession, provided that they take or renew their vows during the Mass.

5. to lay missionaries, in the Mass in which they are publicly sent out on their mission, and to all others in the Mass in which they receive an ecclesiastical mission.

6. in the administration of Viaticum, to a sick person and

to all who are present, when Mass is celebrated in the house of a sick person, in accordance with the existing norms.

7. to a deacon, subdeacon or ministers, who are carrying out their ministry in a solemn or pontifical Mass.

8. when there is a concelebration :
    a) to all who exercise a genuine liturgical function in this concelebration, including lay people, to all seminarians who are present.
    b) in their churches, to all members of Institutes practising the evangelical virtues and to other Societies in which the members, either through religious vows, or solemn commitment or a promise, dedicate themselves to God; and also to all those who normally live in the house of the members of the Institutes and Societies.

9. to priests who take part in big celebrations, but are not able to celebrate or concelebrate.

10. to all groups which are making retreats or following spiritual exercises, in a Mass which is celebrated during the retreat or exercises for those who are taking part; to all those who are taking part in the meeting of some pastoral commission, in the Mass they celebrate in common.

11. to those numbered under nn. 2 and 4, in their Jubilee Masses.

12. to the godfather, godmother, parents and spouse of a baptized adult, together with the lay catechists who have prepared him, in the Mass of the initiation.

13. to the parents, relatives and special benefactors, who take part in the Mass of a newly ordained priest.

'Special benefactors' in this last case should not be interpreted in any strict sense, since otherwise it could make communion under both kinds seem a reward for those who give the biggest donation—not quite the spirit of Christian communion. The basic idea of including 'benefactors' is that the sharing in the joy of a man's ordination should be emphasized and more fully expressed by mutual communion in Christ's body and blood.

Communion in the hand: There is another point regarding reception of communion which is under discussion in some countries at the present time, namely, 'communion in the hand'. This means that instead of the host being placed on the communicant's tongue he takes the eucharistic bread in his hand and then eats it. History shows that 'communion in the hand' was customary throughout the Church until the ninth or tenth century. There is the famous quotation from the *Mystagogic Catecheses* of St Cyril of Jerusalem, where he says : 'When you approach, do not go stretching out your open hands or having your fingers spread out, but make the left hand into a throne for the right which shall receive the King, and then cup your open hand and take the body of Christ, saying *Amen.*' The faithful were expected to wash their hands beforehand and strictly instructed not to misuse the sacrament. The growing emphasis on the divinity of Christ and fears of misuse seem to have been partly responsible for the change here. But

'the change of custom is contemporaneous with the transition from leavened to unleavened bread, and is probably related to it. The delicate pieces of thin wafer almost invited this method of distribution since, unlike the pieces of unleavened bread formerly used, they easily adhered to the moist tongue.'[44]

Recently a number of Episcopal Conferences and individual bishops put in the request that 'communion in the hand' might be permitted in their countries or dioceses. These requests were principally from north-western and central Europe—the same countries in which the liturgical revival had its origins. Before replying to the requests, Pope Paul decided to ask the opinion of all the bishops of the Latin Rite upon this point. The views of the bishops were as follows :

to the question whether reception in the hand should be authorized in just the same way as the present way of distributing communion, the bishops replied—yes, 567; no, 1233; yes with reservations, 315.

to the question whether 'communion in the hand' be permitted in small groups, with permission of the local Ordinary : yes, 751; no, 1215.

[44] Cf Joseph Jungmann, *op. cit.*, p. 510.

to the question whether, after a good catechetical preparation, they thought people would willingly accept the new rite: yes, 835; no, 1185.

These replies show an unmistakable negative on the part of the majority of bishops, and in an Instruction on 29 May 1969, the Congregation of Divine Worship re-affirmed the present usage, which by reason of widely established custom over a long period had attained the status of law. The same Instruction stated, however, that in those countries where 'communion in the hand' already represented a pastoral problem, the Episcopal Conference could—if there was a two-thirds vote in favour—request permission for the 'new' usage in their country. This request has now been made by several countries—such as France and Belgium—and granted by the Holy See.

In the permission given to certain countries regarding this custom, a number of conditions have been laid down by the Congregation for Divine Worship :

1) This method of receiving communion is not to be imposed on the faithful. Each person should feel free to communicate in either the former way or the new way. Both ways can be easily adopted in the same celebration.

2) Careful catechesis must precede its use, so as to show that this in no way conflicts with the Church's eucharistic faith and is a perfectly reasonable way of receiving communion.

3) In receiving communion in this way, the faithful must be aware that it is the Body of Christ that they are receiving, and approach the sacrament with the reverence due to it.

4) The traditional ministerial role of the priest and deacon can be manifested in their placing of the host in the communicant's hand, or the communicant can be allowed to take it directly from the paten or ciborium. In every case, the communicant must consume the host before he returns to his place. The assistance of the ministers is underlined by the usual formula 'the Body of Christ', to which the communicant replies 'Amen'.

5) Care is to be taken lest fragments fall to the floor.

6) In communion under both kinds by intinction, it is never permitted to give communion in the hand.

Two points spring to mind here. As a 'breakdown' of the bishops' voting would probably show, and as the permissions granted by the Holy See illustrate, a certain 'plurality' in the Church's worship is inevitable and even desirable. It is *inevitable* in the sense that to make Orientals think like Westerners, or to impose the thought and behaviour patterns of Latin countries upon those of northern Europe (or vice-versa), is to attempt something which people in the modern world will not accept. Not only will they not accept : they are liable to react with a violence at least the equal of the effort to impose something alien upon them. It is *desirable* in the sense that worship must be an expression of faith in terms of one's own cultural context if it is to be an expression of the whole man. And as the Church of the first four centuries shows us, in a society far less complex and diversified than our own, pluralism does not necessarily destroy unity.

Regarding this particular question of communion in the hand, we should remember that there will be very many in our congregations who were taught so to reverence the host they received in communion that they hardly dared touch it with their teeth, never mind their hand! As one convert said to me, 'Touching the host with my hand, that's blasphemy!' You might say that this is an example of Christian education which confused the essential with the non-essential, and which is partly responsible for much of the disorientation and bewilderment Catholics are experiencing at the present time. Perhaps, but we should take people as we find them, not as we should like or imagine them to be. Just as no amount of rhetoric will compel the modern student to accept something which he thinks is unreasonable, so too, weeks of rationalizing will often have no effect on the emotional attitudes and involvement of half a lifetime. To try and impose 'communion in the hand' therefore on someone who felt it was wrong, would be little short of madness. When people's faith is so closely bound up with the physical expression of this faith, considerable circumspection is required when explaining or presenting changes. This is something which visiting priests— from different countries or areas—could well bear in mind.

A major problem that comes to mind when thinking of communion in the hand is the generation gap. In many spheres of the Church's life, questions and problems that are discussed and debated so laboriously at official level are often non-problems to younger people. Only too often they have already asked the questions, given themselves the answers and moved on. True, this may sometimes be because the problem, or the implications of the problem, have not been understood, but it is not always as simple as that.[45] Many who have had recent experience of group Masses with seminarians or university students, might feel that communion in the hand (and communion under both kinds) is a case in point. They find it hard to see what all the fuss is about, and even harder to understand or accept why—if communion in the hand and under both kinds are theologically sound and strike them as preferable—it should not be permitted.

When celebrating Mass recently in South Germany, I had the opportunity of seeing in practice a parish where the people had been well-prepared and where people received communion either in the usual way or in the hand—without their dividing into groups and factions, and without causing disunity in the congregation. It struck me that here at least the question was not an issue, but both methods were accepted on an equal footing. Most important of all, the stress was on the significance of communion in Christ's body, and on its implication for the community's relationship with God, with one another, and with those outside their own community. When all is said and done, however communion is received or distributed, that is what matters!

In the conflict of views, opinions, and emotional attitudes, which issues of this kind easily arouse, how quickly labels are pinned on people to lambast them the more effectively. On the one hand there are accusations of stifling paternalism, papal imperialism, bourgeois institutionalism and neo-pharisaism; and on the other view, of subjectivism, relativism, modernism, hedonism and neo-Gnosticism, all of which raise a good deal of heat and dust making it difficult to see the wood for the trees.

Christ assured us that the wheat and the cockle would grow side by side until the kingdom was fully revealed, but we might well be more circumspect before we decide what is wheat and what is cockle. For a start, the wheat and the cockle are found in the hearts of each of us and none of us is exempt from the common task of groping forward in the darkness—in a darkness which

---

[45] A shrewd and humorous review of many of the points where the generation gap is keenly felt can be found in Clement J. McNaspy, *Change not Changes*, Paulist Press, New York, 1968.

finally makes us more aware of our absolute need for the life-giving light of Christ. If the members of the Church are going to move forward together, as a community, then there must be give and take.

Ablutions: The rite for the purification of the sacred vessels after communion has been simplified. It is carried out in silence by the priest at the side of the altar or by the deacon at the credence table. If the sacred vessels are purified at the altar, a server afterwards carries them to the credence table. The chalice is purified with wine and then water, or with water alone. The contents of the chalice are then consumed by whoever has carried out the purification. The paten is normally wiped with the purificator (GI, 238). If there is a sub-deacon, he assists the deacon at the credence table and wipes the sacred vessels afterwards (GI, 151).

The sacred vessels, having been covered, can also be left on the altar or preferably on the credence table, and purified after the end of Mass when the people have left the church (GI, 120, 131). In this way more time is available for thanksgiving.

Thanksgiving:

'When the distribution of communion is over, if it is judged to be suitable for the occasion, priest and faithful may pray for a while in silence. If preferred, a hymn, psalm or other song of praise may be sung by the whole assembly' (GI, 56j).

After communion the celebrant can either remain at the altar or go to the seat. If there is to be a period of silent prayer—and this is desirable if circumstances allow—it is best for the priest to leave the ablutions until after the Mass, go to the seat and sit in quiet prayer. The congregation will also sit in silent prayer.

In many places, this period of silent prayer has already been well received. It also meets the desire of the bishops at the 1967 Synod who felt that the Mass should not end too abruptly after communion.

Prayer after communion: In this prayer, the priest prays that the whole assembly may receive the full fruits of the sacrament, and the people make the prayer their own through the acclamation *Amen.*

The prayer may be said either at the altar or at the seat. Omitting 'The Lord be with you', the priest says directly 'Let us pray'. If there has not been a preceding period of silence, the celebrant pauses briefly here before going on with the prayer.

The norms regarding the choice of this prayer are the same as those for the prayer over the gifts. Here too the conclusion will always be the short formula 'Through Christ our Lord'.

4. BLESSING AND DISMISSAL

When the communion rite is over, the Mass moves on to its conclusion.

The 'notices' or 'parish announcement' are in future to be given at this point instead of causing a break between the Gospel and homily (GI, 123, 139). Given the existence of parish notice-boards, bulletins, etc., these notices during the Mass are best kept to a minimum.

After the normal greeting 'the Lord be with you', the celebrant blesses (either said or sung) the assembly in the normal way. On certain days or occasions this blessing is replaced by a more solemn form (e.g. bishop's blessing; blessing at marriages) or by a 'prayer over the people'. These 'prayers over the people', which we still find in Lent, were originally a formula of blessing and they now recover their original usage. These blessings and prayers will be found in the Missal. In explaining these different forms of blessing, it could be pointed out that the words asking God's blessing can be accompanied either by a sign of the cross (the normal form of Christian blessing) or an imposition of hands (as in the prayer over tne people). The important thing is to grasp the significance of both the words and the gestures.

The dismissal, given either by the celebrant or the deacon, is given in the normal way (GI, 124, 140). The new formulas of dismissal 'Go in the peace of Christ', 'The Mass is ended, go in peace', 'Go in peace to love and serve the Lord' are expressive of the Mass's links with the daily life which is to follow.

The priest, and the deacon and sub-deacon if they are present, then kiss the altar (GI, 125, 141, 152). With all the servers they then reverence the altar with a profound bow, or genuflect if the Blessed Sacrament is present in the sanctuary (GI, 233–34).

All these concluding rites (greeting, blessing, dismissal) are omitted when the Mass is immediately followed by another liturgical action (GI, 126). An example of this would be a eucharistic procession (as in the Mass of the Lord's Supper on Maundy (Holy) Thursday), or absolution of the dead—which is now only done when the body is present (GI, 340).

It is important to sing a closing hymn of fitting nature. The celebrant remains at the altar, singing with the people, for some portion of the hymn. On occasion, an instrumental recessional may be equally effective.

The end of Mass will be seen more as a new beginning than an end if the relationship of the Mass to life is understood. This continuity will be underlined if the celebrant and other priests and deacons can find the time to be available and ready to talk with people as they come out of the Church.

CHAPTER VI

Practical Points

1. The Need for Information

The new Order of the Mass is probably less of a 'jolt' for the laity than was the first introduction of the vernacular or the use of vernacular in the canon. Yet there is a risk that if the changes are not explained, many people may be confused and irritated. This will be even more likely if the actual celebration of Sunday Mass is not carefully prepared and clearly presented. Two suggestions might be useful here:

(i) The congregation will normally be very grateful if it is clearly indicated which texts, hymns or prayers are to be used in the celebration of the Mass they are attending. There are many ways of doing this: an announcement from the lectern before Mass begins; a clear statement in the parish bulletin; a notice displayed on a board, similar to that used to give the hymn numbers; an explicit reference in the 'few words' at the beginning of Mass. Practical usefulness aside, this simple courtesy helps the people to feel that the celebration of Mass is intended for them, rather than being something they are merely privileged to observe.

(ii) Over recent years, it has not been easy to supply the congregation with texts or music, since one often wondered whether they would still be in use the following year! Within the next two years it will become easier to supply texts and music assured of a longer life.

141

Given the sheer diversity of tasks that face the pastoral clergy, the growing need for specialization in all fields of pastoral activity, the changing patterns and attitudes of the present time, the nagging concern with administration and finance, and the 1001 things that absorb time and energy in a normal parish, there is more need than ever for effective diocesan programmes by liturgical and music commissions to explain and present liturgical reform. At the very least, these commissions can indicate what texts and music are available; but they can do much more.

2. PRESERVING UNITY AND VARIETY

Besides keeping people well informed as to what is going on and what has proved to be particularly effective and beneficial elsewhere, such commissions can do a great deal in helping to achieve a local balance between *unity* and *variety*.

(i) *Unity*

Where parishes living side by side are at opposite poles of the liturgical spectrum, the situation can be very disruptive of the Church community as a whole. Sometimes one finds that in one parish nothing is happening, and that next door everything and anything is happening! Situations can arise where in one area the pastor/parish priest holds as close as possible to the liturgy as it was before the Council and tries to resist the reform, rather like Canute trying to turn back the incoming tide; whilst nearby the young priest thrusts his latest idea down the throats of the congregation, delights in 'shocking' the greater number, and generally treats the people like a herd of cattle! Caricature as this may be, both attitudes exist at least in part and are characterized by insensitivity to the people to whom one is ministering; both are forms of clericalism which we could very well do without. As a bishop remarked during the Council, 'It's fine calling ourselves shepherds—as long as we don't treat the people like sheep!'

It is here that a diocesan commission—with the backing of the bishop, the synod of priests and the pastoral council—can help to establish a general pattern throughout the diocese, perhaps in keeping with the general pattern throughout the country. But unity does not mean uniformity, and there must be flexibility. A cathedral, for instance, has greater resources and possibilities than a country parish; moreover, it must meet different needs. To expect every parish to produce exactly the same liturgical pattern is not only undesirable but actually impossible. In the last resort, one can only appeal to people's common sense to achieve the right balance.

(ii) *Variety*

The new Order of the Mass offers many possibilities. Diocesan commissions can do a great deal in encouraging imaginative use of the variety that is provided. The preparation of a living liturgy always demands hard work, and this is probably even more necessary with the new Mass.

Normally, there are varying degrees of solemnity at parish Masses, according to the time of celebration : more or less singing, with or without a choir, various types of music, number of ministers and servers, the use of incense, type of vestments, etc. Surely it is desirable that there should be this variety. But many church-goers come to Mass at the same time on a Sunday, be it 8 a.m., 11 a.m. or 7 p.m. It is very important then that there should be variety even *within* these Masses. The new Order offers many possibilities which, when clearly presented and explained, will help avoid monotony and engage the congregation's attention more easily. Skilful use of these alternatives will also help to deepen understanding and participation in the Mass.

Take a concrete example : *the eucharistic prayers*. The Consilium recommended that the Roman Canon and Eucharistic Prayer III be used on Sundays. The reason is clear : to ensure that the Prefaces which are proper to the season or feast be fully used. But that does not mean that the other eucharistic prayers cannot or should not be used on Sundays! On the contrary, the purpose of introducing alternatives to the Roman Canon was to enable us all to become more aware of the riches of the eucharist and to understand more fully its place in our lives. This purpose cannot be achieved by relegating Eucharistic Prayers II and IV to weekday Masses. It is perfectly legitimate to use these prayers on those Sundays or feasts which do not have a preface which is *strictly* proper. (A preface is considered proper in the strict sense in Masses celebrated on the *feast day itself* or in the octave of a feast.) In fact it is desirable. Reports seem to show that where it has been used, the fourth eucharistic prayer has been the most popular of the four. Experience has shown that while it is true that congregations with 'a deeper biblical knowledge' are more aware of its content and significance, this does not mean that it is not appreciated or understood by other congregations.

An important point to note here is that those publishers who provide the valuable service of printed leaflets for use by the congregation Sunday by Sunday, should not stick to exactly the same form every Sunday. They should vary the eucharistic prayer, the penitential rite and those other parts of the Mass where flexibility and variety have been deliberately provided. This should be done in consultation with the national, regional or diocesan commission, as the case may be.

Obviously we are not suggesting here such rapidity of change and variation that people do not know whether they are coming or going. Some variation however—carefully prepared, spaced out—are an essential feature of the new liturgy. The rigidity of former distinctions between this and that type of Mass has gone. The way is now open to that variety best suited to local needs.

Two further examples where variation can be effective are in the use of music and the use of silence.

We have spoken earlier of the importance of *music* in helping to make the celebration of Mass a humanly attractive experience. Given the right conditions it can have a livening effect on the celebration, which really can be compared with the way yeast makes bread rise. In the new Order of Mass, there are endless possibilities regarding singing and music, with and without a choir, and as has already been pointed out, certain parts of the Mass are primarily intended to be sung.

But what of people unaccustomed to singing?

'Singing is only worthwhile when it is done with conviction. Many other activities can be adequately carried out from a sense of duty, but not singing. If people make an effort to sing merely because they are instructed to do so, then the battle is already lost. In dealing with people who have been unaccustomed to singing, there must first of all be a process of conversion, whereby they come to regard singing as completely natural and desirable. This change of heart can only be produced in them by one who is himself convinced. This kind of leadership is absolutely indispensable and, though requiring no specifically musical gifts, without it the efforts of organists, choirmasters and others will be in vain. These provide the "know-how"; but in practice there is no substitute for the enthusiastic initiative of the parish clergy."[1]

Coupled with this, some form of leadership during the celebration itself will normally be necessary, whether this is given by cantor, choir, choirmaster or organist. Theory must always be equated with practical possibility : 'Common sense should be exercised in both the amount and difficulty of the music that congregations are required to master in a given time. "Less rather than more" is practically and psychologically better.'[1]

The General Instruction underlines the value of *silence* as an intrinsic part of the celebration. The nature of the silence differs according to the part of the Mass: in the penitential act and after the invitation to pray at the beginning of the Collect, each person becomes aware of himself in God's presence; after the readings or homily, brief silent meditation on what has been heard can be very fruitful; silence during the preparation of the gifts can offer a useful psychological break as the assembly sits quietly after the liturgy of the word and prepares for the eucharistic prayer; praise and thanksgiving come naturally after communion, both in silence and in song.

3. BEING SEEN AND HEARD

To what use all the rest if sight and sound are not available? Liturgy is a language of signs : symbols, words, gestures. Can the gestures be seen? Can the celebrant, reader or cantor be heard?

These are basic practical points that must be established, yet are often overlooked. A few points are offered briefly here, but the question merits further attention, especially in the training of priests and lay readers.[2]

[1] The National Commission for Catholic Church Music in England and Wales (ed.), *Music in the Mass,* C.T.S., London, p. 7, art. 17; p. 8, art. 22.

[2] A more thorough treatment of this subject may be found in Raymond Clarke, *Sounds Effective,* Geoffrey Chapman, London 1969.

(i)   The first point to notice is that the celebrant's own attitude will greatly affect the way he says and does things on the sanctuary. He is the leader of the assembly, and the way the celebration develops will to a large extent depend on him. The first requisite is a living faith, sensitive awareness, commitment :

> 'If you ask what this has to do with style and presence in celebration, I would answer "everything—absolutely everything!" Commitment, personal commitment, the personal conviction that the Gospel and the Church and the sacraments are all together an inseparable and utterly necessary good in the life of man and his world—this is the very first requirement and the fundament of all.'[3]

This attitude will be expressed in the concern of the celebrant. A group of dockers said about their parochial clergy in the East End of London, 'You know what it is about our priests, Father? *They care!*' This concern is shown in the attention the celebrant gives the people, and as Robert Hovda remarked, 'You can't give people any real attention in the eucharistic hall if you haven't given them attention before they arrive'.[4]

(ii)   The second point follows from the above : as leader of the assembly, the celebrant's stance should be relaxed and natural, but with quiet dignity. Just as arrogance is out of place, so too is timidity and embarrassment. Hovda puts it well when he says of the priest : 'He is a free man who has chosen to be Christ's man, and this is what his carriage must convey'.[5]

All the actions of the celebrant must be directed towards the purpose of the liturgy, and whether he is standing or sitting, speaking or listening, he should be helping the congregation to participate, leading them into the action itself. When listening to the readings, for example, he should give the lead in actually listening. Likewise in the silence after communion, he himself must be still and pray in silence.

---

[3] Robert W. Hovda, 'Style and Presence in Celebration', *Worship* 41 (1967), p. 516.
[4] *Ibid.,* p. 520.
[5] *Ibid.,* p. 521.

(iii)   The way a priest wears vestments will to some extent express his attitude to the celebration of Mass, and reflect his respect for the people who have come to join in the celebration with him. The way a priest moves around the sanctuary will also affect the congregation. No one wants the celebrant to look as though he just stepped out of a stained-glass window. Artificiality is contrary to that worship in spirit and truth which must be the hallmark of Christian liturgy—but slovenliness and haste are equally out of place. In the present writer's experience, the comments of honest friends in this regard can be a sobering experience. But there are defects here that others can see more clearly than oneself—has the genuflection become a mere bob, with the altar as a prop? Is the sign of the cross recognizable as such?

'A gesture is a physical expression of thought. It underlines what the mind is thinking and the voice is saying, and as such it also reacts on the tone of the voice.'[6]

Gestures should be easy and natural rather than jerky or stiff, and particularly in the homily celebrants should avoid letting gestures become something like a nervous twitch or personal idiosyncrasy. In the homily, economy of gesture is more likely to be effective than a flurry of arms, continual wagging of fingers and shaking of head.

(iv)   If the use of voice is to be effective, there are a number of things to bear in mind :

a)   *Audibility:* to achieve this, the speaker must have enough breath and be relaxed enough to allow the chest, throat and mouth to give good resonance.

b)   *Clarity:*

'If your speech sounds are indistinct, slurred, half-swallowed, clipped short, muffled or merged with adjoining words, you need to practise enunciation. Good enunciation depends on four factors : jaw, lips, tongue and teeth. A locked jaw and lazy lips are the usual problems. Make sure that your lips are wide enough so that you sound the word properly. In public

---

[6] Raymond Clarke, *op. cit.*, p. 28.

speaking situations you will find that you must make your jaw, lips, tongue and teeth function with greater deliberation and effort.'[7]

c) *Tone:* it is extremely important to avoid a monotonous tone of voice. There is no surer way of 'turning people off'. Most people, too, are very much averse to a 'churchy voice'. It is extraordinary sometimes to see the way a man's voice can change when he has to speak publicly in church, and the only way to overcome this is to practise in front of a group of unsparing critics until the defect is overcome. People are much happier if they can recognize the voice used at the lectern as the same as that used when away from the lectern and outside the church. Variation in tone, change of pitch, colourful inflection— these must relate to the meaning of what is being said and help to bring out that meaning. With practice you can also make use of the natural 'pitch' of the building you are in.[8] Through practice, a tone can be achieved which is neither hard nor clinical nor sentimental, but which helps engage the listeners' attention and draws them to understand what is being said.

d) *Pace:* This must be adjusted to the size and acoustics of the building in which one is speaking. The normal tendency is to speak too rapidly. Variations in pace and skilful use of the pause are indispensable assets to public speaking.

(v) Care must be taken with regard to reading in church.

'When the reader reads the Word of God, he must proclaim that Word. This means that he needs to give the reading all the solemnity and richness that is contained in the sacred text. It does not mean that he becomes pompous or over-dramatic. But it does mean that he communicates to the audience from the printed page the sacred word in its fullness of thought, feeling and beauty. He is to communicate with his voice and his entire body. His whole presentation must convey the effect which the sacred author intended. The reader then is a re-creative artist.'[9]

[7] *Techniques for reading and commentation*, Liturgy Training Program, Archdiocese of Chicago, 1967.
[8] Raymond Clarke, *op. cit.*, p. 59.
[9] Chicago Liturgy Training Program, *op. cit.*

A number of points come up here :

a) Preparation of the reading is an absolute 'must'; it is usually only too evident when the reading has not been prepared.

b) The first object of the preparation should be to understand what you are going to read, and determine the literary genre. Is it verse? Prose? Narrative? Dialogue? Is the mood reflective? Vigorous? Gentle? etc. There are further questions : where should the pauses come? Where is emphasis required? Is the lectern at the right height? If not, can it be adjusted?

c) If there is a microphone, nothing can replace on the spot practice. What has been said about pitch, enunciation and pace are just as true with a microphone as without one.

d) Stand still :

'Stillness is vital for any speaker. If there is stillness then it is easy for full attention to be paid to the words without their being blunted by irrelevant movements. If a speaker is continually moving, the listener eventually ends by watching the movements rather than listening to what is being said.'[10]

[10] Raymond Clarke, *op. cit.*, p. 31.

APPENDIX

Rubrics from the General Instruction to the New Order of Mass[1]

77. Mass with the people is understood as that which is celebrated with the participation of the people. As far as possible it is fitting, especially on Sundays and holy days of obligation, that the celebration should be carried out with singing and a suitable number of ministers. However it may also be carried out without singing and with only one minister (server).

78. Besides the celebrating priest there should normally be a lector, cantor, and at least one minister (server): in what follows this will be referred to as the 'typical' form of Mass. But the rite which is described below also makes provision for a greater number of ministers.

   Whatever form the celebration takes, there may always be a deacon exercising his office.

Items to be prepared

79. The altar should be covered with at least one altar-cloth. On it or by the side of it there are placed at least two candle-sticks with lighted candles in them, but there can

---

[1] Numbers refer to the paragraphs of the General Instruction.

also be four, six, or, if the bishop of the diocese is celebrating the Mass, seven candlesticks with lighted candles. There should be a cross either on the altar or not too distant from it. The candlesticks and cross may be brought in with the entrance procession. The book of the Gospels, if distinct from the book with the other readings, may also be placed ready on the altar, unless it is to be brought in with the entrance procession.

80. On the sanctuary there should be :
   a) near the presidential chair : the Missal (or Sacramentary or Book of Collects), and, if desired, the book of songs and chants;
   b) on the lectern : the lectionary;
   c) on the credence table : chalice, corporal, purificator, and, if desired, the pall; the paten and ciboriums, if these last are necessary, with the bread for the communion of priest, ministers, and people; the cruets with wine and water, unless all these are to be presented by the people in the presentation of the gifts : and those items which are necessary for washing of hands. The chalice is covered with a veil, which may always be white in colour.

81. In the sacristy, the vestments for the priest and ministers are prepared according to the requirements of the various forms of celebration :
   a) for the priest : alb, stole and chasuble;
   b) for the deacon : alb, stole and dalmatic. Whether by necessity or by reason of the lesser degree of solemnity, the dalmatic can also be omitted;
   c) for the subdeacon : alb and tunicle. This tunicle may also be omitted for the same reasons as the deacon may omit the dalmatic;
   d) for the other ministers (servers) : albs or cottas.

All those who wear albs use girdles (cinctures) and amices, unless desired otherwise.

I. Mass Celebrated With the People

Introductory Rites

82. When the people have assembled, the priest and ministers, wearing their vestments, proceed to the altar in the following order :
    a) a minister with thurible, if incense is to be used;
    b) the ministers who, if desired, carry torches, and among them, if there is to be one, a minister with the cross; and the other ministers who are present;
    c) the lector, who can also carry in the book of the Gospels;
    d) the priest who is to celebrate the Mass.

    If incense is to be used the priest puts some into the thurible before the procession begins.

83. The entrance song is executed during the procession to the altar (cf nos. 25–6).

84. When they reach the altar the priest and ministers make a profound bow, or, if there is a tabernacle with the Blessed Sacrament present, they genuflect.

    If the cross has been brought in with the procession, it is placed near the altar or in some other suitable place; the candlesticks brought in with the procession are placed either near the altar or on the credence-table; the book of Gospels is placed on the altar.

85. The priest goes up to the altar and venerates it with a kiss. Then, if desired, he may incense the altar.

86. Afterwards the priest goes to the presidential chair. When the entrance song is completed, and with all standing, both priest and people make the sign of the cross. The priest says : *In nomine Patris, et Filii, et Spiritus Sancti.* The people reply : *Amen.*

    Facing the people and extending his hands, the priest then greets them, using one of the formulas provided for this purpose. Either he or some other suitable minister may also introduce the faithful to the Mass of the day with a few brief words.

87. After the penitential act, the *Kyrie* and *Gloria* are said in accordance with the rubrics (nos. 30–1). The *Gloria* may

be intoned either by the priest himself or by cantors, or
may be begun by all together

88. The priest, with his hands joined, then invites the people
to pray, saying: *Oremus.* And for a short time all pray in
silence together with the priest. With his hands extended the
priest then says the prayer, and when it is finished the
people say: *Amen.*

The Liturgy of the Word

89. When the prayer is over, the lector goes to the lectern and
reads the first reading. The whole assembly sits and listens,
and responds with the acclamation at the end of the reading.

90. When the reading has finished, a psalmist, or a cantor, or
the lector himself, sings or recites the psalm, with the people
singing or saying the response (cf no. 36).

91. Afterwards, if there is to be a second reading before the
Gospel, the lector reads it at the lectern as above, with the
whole assembly sitting, listening and coming in with the
acclamation at the end.

92. The *Alleluia* or another song follows, according to the
requirements of the liturgical season (cf nos. 37–9).

93. If incense is to be used the priest puts it into the thurible
while the *Alleluia* or other song is being sung. Then, with
hands joined and bowing towards the altar, he says silently:
Munda cor meum.

94. He then takes the book of the Gospels if it is on the altar,
and preceded by the ministers, who may carry incense and
torches, goes to the lectern.

95. At the lectern the priest opens the book and says: *Dominus
vobiscum,* and then *Initium* or *Sequentia,* signing the book
with his thumb, and signing his own forehead, mouth and
breast. If desired, he then incenses the book. After the
people's acclamation he proclaims the Gospel, and when
it is finished he kisses the Gospel, saying silently: *Per
evangelica dicta deleantur nostra delicta.* After the Gospel
there is an acclamation of the people, according to the
customs of the region.

96. If there is no lector, the priest himself reads all the readings,
and, if necessary, the songs between the readings, standing

at the lectern. Likewise, if incense is to be used he puts it into the thurible. At the *Munda cor meum* he bows towards the altar.

97. The homily is given either at the chair or at the lectern.

98. The Creed is said by the priest together with the people (cf no. 44). At the words *Et incarnatus est, etc.,* all bow; on the feasts of the Annunciation and Christmas all genuflect at this point.

99. The universal prayer or the prayer of the faithful (bidding prayers) follows, with the people taking an active part. The priest leads the prayer either from the chair or from the lectern (cf nos. 45–7).

EUCHARISTIC LITURGY

100. When the prayers of the faithful have finished, the offertory song begins (cf no. 50). The ministers place the corporal, purificator, chalice and missal on the altar.

101. It is fitting that the participation of the people should be manifested through the presentation of the bread and wine for the eucharistic celebration, and of other gifts by which the needs of the church and poor are provided for.

The offerings of the faithful are fittingly received by the priest with the assistance of the ministers, and put in a suitable place; the bread and wine for the Eucharist however are taken to the altar.

102. At the altar, the priest takes the paten with the bread from the minister, and holds it with both hands above the altar, saying the formula provided. He then places the paten with the bread on the corporal.

103. Afterwards, standing at the side of the altar, he pours wine and a little water into the chalice, saying silently the prescribed formula, and with a minister holding the cruets. Having returned to the middle of the altar, he takes the chalice with both hands and holds it above the altar, while saying the formula provided. He then places the chalice on the corporal, and, if desired, covers it with the pall.

104. Having placed the chalice on the corporal, the priest bows and says silently : *In spiritu humilitatis.*

105. The priest may also incense the gifts and the altar, and a minister (server) may incense the priest and people.

106. After the prayer *In spiritu humilitatis* or after the incensation, the priest, standing at the side of the altar, washes his hands, saying the prescribed formula silently, while the minister pours the water.

107. Having returned to the middle of the altar, standing facing the people, extending and joining his hands, the priest invites the people to pray, saying: *Orate, fratres, etc.* After the people's response, he says, with his hands extended, the prayer over the gifts. At the end of this the people say: *Amen.*

108. The priest then begins the eucharistic prayer. Extending his hands he says: *Dominus vobiscum.* As he goes on to say: *Sursum corda,* he raises his hands; then, with hands extended, he adds: *Gratias agamus Domino Deo nostro.* After the people's response: *Dignum et iustum est,* the priest goes on to the preface. When that is finished, with his hands joined he sings or says in a loud voice together with the ministers and people: *Sanctus-Benedictus* (cf no. 55b).

109. The priest continues with the eucharistic prayer in accordance with the rubrics given in each of the prayers.

110. After the doxology which closes the eucharistic prayer, the priest, with hands joined, says the introduction to the Lord's prayer, and then, with his hands extended, says the Lord's prayer together with the people.

111. Following the Lord's prayer, the priest alone, with his hands extended, says the embolism: *Libera nos.* The people respond: *Quia tuum est regnum.*

112. Then the priest says in a loud voice the prayer: *Domine Iesu Christe, qui dixisti;* when that is finished, extending and joining his hands, he expresses a greeting of peace, saying: *Pax Domini sit semper vobiscum.* The people reply: *Et cum spiritu tuo.* Afterwards, if desired, the priest adds: *Offerte vobis pacem.* And all, in accordance with the customs of the region, make a gesture which expresses mutual peace and charity. The priest can make this gesture of peace with the ministers.

113. Afterwards the priest takes the host, breaks it over the paten,

and puts a particle in the chalice, saying silently: *Haec commixtio.* Meanwhile the *Agnus Dei* is sung or said by the choir and people (cf no. 56c).

114. The priest then says silently the prayer: *Domine Iesu Christe, Fili Dei vivi* or *Perceptio Corporis et Sanguinis.*

115. After this prayer, the priest genuflects, takes the host, and holding it slightly elevated above the paten, says facing the people: *Ecce Agnus Dei,* and together with the people adds: *Domine, non sum dignus.*

116. Afterwards, standing facing the altar, the priest says silently: *Corpus Christi custodiat me in vitam aeternam,* and reverently receives the body of Christ. Then he takes the chalice and says: *Sanguis Christi custodiat me in vitam aeternam,* and reverently receives the blood of Christ.

117. He then takes the paten or ciborium, and goes to those who are to receive comunion. Holding the host slightly elevated, he shows it to each person as he says: *Corpus Christi.* The communicant replies: *Amen,* and receives the sacrament.

118. For communion under both kinds, that rite is followed which is described in another part of the General Instruction (cf no. 240–52).

119. While the priest receives the sacrament, the communion song begins (cf no. 56i).

120. After the distribution of communion, the priest, having returned to the altar, collects the fragments which remain. Standing at the side of the altar he then purifies the paten or ciborium over the chalice, afterwards purifying the chalice and wiping the chalice with the purificator. The purified vessels are carried by the minister to the credence-table. It is however permitted, particularly if there are a number of sacred vessels to be purified, to leave the vessels on the altar or at the credence on a corporal (the vessels may be covered if this seems more desirable) and to purify them after Mass is over.

121. When the ablutions are over the priest can go to the presidential chair. A period of silence can be observed, with the whole assembly seated, or a psalm or canticle of praise may be used (cf no. 56k).

122. Afterwards, standing at the chair or at the altar, the priest says, facing the people: *Oremus,* and, with his hands

extended, says the prayer after communion, before which there may be a short pause of silence, unless there has already been a period of silence after communion. At the end of the prayer, the people say : *Amen.*

CONCLUDING RITES

123. If there are to be parish notices or announcements of any kind, they are given after the postcommunion prayer.
124. Then the priest, extending his hands, greets the people, saying : *Dominus vobiscum,* to which the people respond : *Et cum spiritu tuo.* The priest immediately adds : *Benedicat vos omnipotens Deus,* and, blessing them with a sign of the cross, says : *Pater, et Filius, et Spiritus Sanctus. Amen.* On certain days and occasions, another formula of blessing takes the place of this in accordance with the rubrics, be it a more solemn form of blessing, or a prayer over the people.

    Immediately after the blessing, the priest, with his hands joined, adds : *Ite, missa est*; and all reply : *Deo gratias.*
125. Then the priest venerates the altar with a kiss. After a due reverence together with the ministers, he then goes out.
126. If Mass is followed by another liturgical function, the concluding rites, namely the greeting, blessing and dismissal, are omitted.

II. MASS WITHOUT THE PEOPLE

GENERAL POINTS

209. We are dealing here with a Mass celebrated by a priest, with only one server assisting and responding.
210. This type of Mass follows in its general lines the Mass celebrated with the people, with the server, if opportune, answering with the responses of the people.
211. Mass is to be celebrated without a server only in cases of serious necessity. In this case the greetings and the blessing at the end of Mass are omitted.
212. The chalice is prepared before Mass either on a credence-table near the altar, or on the altar itself. The Missal is placed at the left side of the altar.

Introductory Rites

213. The priest, having reverenced the altar, makes the sign of the cross over himself, saying : *In nomine Patris, etc.* Facing the server, he greets him, using one of the formulas provided, and, standing at the foot of the altar, carries out the act of penance or the penitential act.

214. He then goes up to the altar and venerates it with a kiss; he goes immediately to the Missal on the left-hand side of the altar, where he remains until the end of the prayers of the faithful.

215. He then reads the entrance antiphon, and says the *Kyrie* and *Gloria* in accordance with the rubrics.

216. With his hands joined, he says *Oremus* and, after a short pause, extends his hands and says the prayer. At the end the server says : *Amen.*

Liturgy of the Word

217. When he has said the prayer, the server or the priest himself reads the first reading and the psalm, and, when it is to be said, the second reading together with the *Alleluia* verse or other versicle.

218. Remaining in the same place, the priest bows and says the *Munda cor meum,* and reads the Gospel. At the end, he venerates the book with a kiss, saying silently : *Per evangelica dicta, etc.* The server says the response.

219. If the Creed is to be used at that Mass according to the rubrics, the priest then says it together with the server.

220. The prayers of the faithful may then follow even in this Mass. The priest says the intentions and the server replies.

Eucharistic Liturgy

221. The Offertory antiphon is omitted. The server places the corporal, purificator and chalice on the altar, unless they have already been put there at the beginning of Mass.

222. The placing of the bread and wine on the altar, and the

mixing of the water and wine are carried out in the same way as in Masses celebrated with the people, using the formulas assigned in the Order of the Mass. After the deposition of the bread and wine the priest washes his hands, standing at the side of the altar and with the server pouring the water.

223. The priest says the prayer over the gifts and the eucharistic prayer, using the rite described for Mass with the people.

224. The Lord's prayer with its embolism is said as in Masses with the people.

225. After the acclamation at the end of the embolism, the priest says the prayer *Domine Iesu Christe, qui dixisti*; and he then adds : *Pax Domini sit semper vobiscum,* to which the server replies : *Et cum spiritu tuo.* If considered opportune the priest may also give the 'pax' to the server.

226. Then, while he says the *Agnus Dei* with the server, the priest breaks the host over the paten. After the *Agnus Dei,* he places a particle of the host in the chalice, saying : *Haec commixtio.*

227. The priest then goes on to say silently the prayer *Domine Iesu Christe, Fili Dei vivi* or *Perceptio.* He then genuflects, takes the host, and, if the server is to receive communion, holding the host slightly above the paten and facing the server, he says : *Ecce Agnus Dei,* and says with him once : *Domine, non sum dignus.* Facing the altar he then receives the body of Christ. If the server is not in fact receiving communion, the priest takes the host, and, facing the altar, says silently : *Domine, non sum dignus,* and receives the body of Christ. The receiving of the blood of Christ is carried out in the same way as described already in Mass with the people.

228. Before he gives communion to the server, the priest says the communion antiphon.

229. The purification of the chalice is done at the side of the altar. Then the chalice may either be carried by the server to the credence-table, or, as at the beginning, be left on the altar.

230. After the purification of the chalice, the priest may have a pause of silence. Afterwards he says the prayer after communion.

Concluding Rites

231. The concluding rites are carried out in the same way as in Mass with the people, except that the *Ite, missa est* is omitted.